All-in-One Planner for 2015:

Yearly

Monthly

Weekly

Daily

By Alicorn Publishing

Alicorn Publishing

All-in-One Planner for 2015: Yearly, Monthly, Weekly, Daily / Alicorn Publishing

ISBN-13: 978-0-9864297-0-5

ISBN-10: 0-9864297-0-5

Table of Contents

Part One

Personal Information   1

Part Two

Yearly Planner 2015-2016   5

Part Three

Monthly Planner 2015   13

Part Four

Weekly Planner 2015   39

Part Five

Daily Planner 2015   147

Part Six

Notes Section   519

Part One

Personal Information

❖ Owner's contact information if book is lost

❖ Emergency contact information

Personal Information

Owner's Name_____

Address_____

_____

City_____

State_____ Zip_____

Phone_____

Cell_____

Email_____

_____

Business/ Organization Name_____

_____

Address_____

_____

City_____

State_____ Zip_____

Work Phone_____

Work Cell_____

Work Email_____

_____

Personal Information

Emergency Contact_____

Relationship_____

Address_____

_____

City_____

State_____ Zip_____

Phone_____

Cell_____

Email_____

_____

Emergency Contact_____

Relationship_____

Address_____

_____

City_____

State_____ Zip_____

Phone_____

Cell_____

Email_____

_____

Part Two
Yearly Planner
2015-2016

Great for long-term planning:

- ❖ Project planning
- ❖ Fund-raising
- ❖ Academic deadlines

Year 2015

JAN 2015

S	M	T	W	R	F	S
				1	2	3
4	5	6	7	8	9	10
11	12	13	14	15	16	17
18	19	20	21	22	23	24
25	26	27	28	29	30	31

FEB 2015

S	M	T	W	R	F	S
1	2	3	4	5	6	7
8	9	10	11	12	13	14
15	16	17	18	19	20	21
22	23	24	25	26	27	28

MAR 2015

S	M	T	W	R	F	S
1	2	3	4	5	6	7
8	9	10	11	12	13	14
15	16	17	18	19	20	21
22	23	24	25	26	27	28
29	30	31				

APR 2015

S	M	T	W	R	F	S
			1	2	3	4
5	6	7	8	9	10	11
12	13	14	15	16	17	18
19	20	21	22	23	24	25
26	27	28	29	30		

MAY 2015

S	M	T	W	R	F	S
					1	2
3	4	5	6	7	8	9
10	11	12	13	14	15	16
17	18	19	20	21	22	23
24	25	26	27	28	29	30
31						

Planning Notes 2015

_____
_____
_____
_____
_____
_____
_____
_____
_____
_____
_____
_____
_____
_____
_____
_____
_____
_____
_____
_____
_____
_____
_____
_____
_____
_____
_____
_____
_____
_____
_____
_____
_____
_____
_____
_____
_____

Year 2015

JUN 2015						
S	M	T	W	R	F	S
	1	2	3	4	5	6
7	8	9	10	11	12	13
14	15	16	17	18	19	20
21	22	23	24	25	26	27
28	29	30				

JULY 2015						
S	M	T	W	R	F	S
			1	2	3	4
5	6	7	8	9	10	11
12	13	14	15	16	17	18
19	20	21	22	23	24	25
26	27	28	29	30	31	

AUG 2015						
S	M	T	W	R	F	S
						1
2	3	4	5	6	7	8
9	10	11	12	13	14	15
16	17	18	19	20	21	22
23	24	25	26	27	28	29
30	31					

SEP 2015						
S	M	T	W	R	F	S
		1	2	3	4	5
6	7	8	9	10	11	12
13	14	15	16	17	18	19
20	21	22	23	24	25	26
27	28	29	30			

OCT 2015						
S	M	T	W	R	F	S
				1	2	3
4	5	6	7	8	9	10
11	12	13	14	15	16	17
18	19	20	21	22	23	24
25	26	27	28	29	30	31

Planning Notes 2015

Year 2015

NOV 2015						
S	M	T	W	R	F	S
1	2	3	4	5	6	7
8	9	10	11	12	13	14
15	16	17	18	19	20	21
22	23	24	25	26	27	28
29	30					

DEC 2015						
S	M	T	W	R	F	S
		1	2	3	4	5
6	7	8	9	10	11	12
13	14	15	16	17	18	19
20	21	22	23	24	25	26
27	28	29	30	31		

Observances 2015

Jan 1	New Year's Day
Jan 19	Martin Luther King Jr. Day
Feb 14	Valentine's Day
Feb 16	Presidents' Day
Feb 17	Mardi Gras
Mar 8	Daylight Saving Time Starts
Mar 20	Spring Equinox
Apr 3	Good Friday
Apr 5	Easter Sunday
Apr 6	Easter Monday
Apr 15	Tax Day
May 10	Mothers' Day
May 25	Memorial Day
Jun 21	Summer Solstice
Jun 21	Father's Day
July 4	Independence Day
Sep 7	Labor Day
Sep 23	Fall Equinox
Oct 12	Columbus Day
Oct 31	Halloween
Nov 1	Daylight Saving Time Ends
Nov 11	Veterans' Day
Nov 26	Thanksgiving Day
Dec 21	Winter Solstice
Dec 25	Christmas Day
Dec 31	New Year's Eve

Planning Notes 2015

Year 2016

JAN 2016

S	M	T	W	R	F	S
					1	2
3	4	5	6	7	8	9
10	11	12	13	14	15	16
17	18	19	20	21	22	23
24	25	26	27	28	29	30
31						

FEB 2016

S	M	T	W	R	F	S
	1	2	3	4	5	6
7	8	9	10	11	12	13
14	15	16	17	18	19	20
21	22	23	24	25	26	27
28	29					

MAR 2016

S	M	T	W	R	F	S
		1	2	3	4	5
6	7	8	9	10	11	12
13	14	15	16	17	18	19
20	21	22	23	24	25	26
27	28	29	30	31		

APR 2016

S	M	T	W	R	F	S
					1	2
3	4	5	6	7	8	9
10	11	12	13	14	15	16
17	18	19	20	21	22	23
24	25	26	27	28	29	30

MAY 2016

S	M	T	W	R	F	S
1	2	3	4	5	6	7
8	9	10	11	12	13	14
15	16	17	18	19	20	21
22	23	24	25	26	27	28
29	30	31				

Planning Notes 2016

Year 2016

JUN 2016						
S	M	T	W	R	F	S
			1	2	3	4
5	6	7	8	9	10	11
12	13	14	15	16	17	18
19	20	21	22	23	24	25
26	27	28	29	30		

JULY 2016						
S	M	T	W	R	F	S
					1	2
3	4	5	6	7	8	9
10	11	12	13	14	15	16
17	18	19	20	21	22	23
24	25	26	27	28	29	30
31						

AUG 2016						
S	M	T	W	R	F	S
	1	2	3	4	5	6
7	8	9	10	11	12	13
14	15	16	17	18	19	20
21	22	23	24	25	26	27
28	29	30	31			

SEP 2016						
S	M	T	W	R	F	S
				1	2	3
4	5	6	7	8	9	10
11	12	13	14	15	16	17
18	19	20	21	22	23	24
25	26	27	28	29	30	

OCT 2016						
S	M	T	W	R	F	S
						1
2	3	4	5	6	7	8
9	10	11	12	13	14	15
16	17	18	19	20	21	22
23	24	25	26	27	28	29
30	31					

Planning Notes 2016

Year 2016

NOV 2016						
S	M	T	W	R	F	S
		1	2	3	4	5
6	7	8	9	10	11	12
13	14	15	16	17	18	19
20	21	22	23	24	25	26
27	28	29	30			

DEC 2016						
S	M	T	W	R	F	S
				1	2	3
4	5	6	7	8	9	10
11	12	13	14	15	16	17
18	19	20	21	22	23	24
25	26	27	28	29	30	31

Observances 2016

Jan 1	New Year's Day
Jan 18	Martin Luther King Jr. Day
Feb 9	Mardi Gras
Feb 14	Valentine's Day
Feb 15	Presidents' Day
Mar 13	Daylight Saving Time Starts
Mar 19	Spring Equinox
Mar 25	Good Friday
Mar 27	Easter Sunday
Mar 28	Easter Monday
Apr 15	Tax Day
May 8	Mothers' Day
May 30	Memorial Day
Jun 19	Fathers' Day
Jun 20	Summer Solstice
July 4	Independence Day
Sep 5	Labor Day
Sep 22	Fall Equinox
Oct 10	Columbus Day
Oct 31	Halloween
Nov 6	Daylight Saving Time Ends
Nov 11	Veterans' Day
Nov 24	Thanksgiving Day
Dec 21	Winter Solstice
Dec 25	Christmas Day
Dec 31	New Year's Eve

Planning Notes 2016

Part Three
Monthly Planner
2015

❖ See dates and plans
at-a-glance

January 2015

Sunday	Monday	Tuesday	Wednesday
4	5	6	7
11	12	13	14
18	19	20	21
25	26	27	28

Thursday	Friday	Saturday	Notes
1_____	2_____	3_____	_____
_____	_____	_____	_____
_____	_____	_____	_____
_____	_____	_____	_____
_____	_____	_____	_____
_____	_____	_____	_____
8_____	9_____	10_____	_____
_____	_____	_____	_____
_____	_____	_____	_____
_____	_____	_____	_____
_____	_____	_____	_____
_____	_____	_____	_____
15_____	16_____	17_____	_____
_____	_____	_____	_____
_____	_____	_____	_____
_____	_____	_____	_____
_____	_____	_____	_____
_____	_____	_____	_____
22_____	23_____	24_____	_____
_____	_____	_____	_____
_____	_____	_____	_____
_____	_____	_____	_____
_____	_____	_____	_____
_____	_____	_____	_____
29_____	30_____	31_____	_____
_____	_____	_____	_____
_____	_____	_____	_____
_____	_____	_____	_____
_____	_____	_____	_____

February 2015

Sunday	Monday	Tuesday	Wednesday
1	2	3	4
8	9	10	11
15	16	17	18
22	23	24	25

February 2015

Thursday	Friday	Saturday	Notes
5	6	7	
12	13	14	
19	20	21	
26	27	28	

March 2015

Sunday	Monday	Tuesday	Wednesday
1	2	3	4
8	9	10	11
15	16	17	18
22	23	24	25
29	30	31	

March 2015

Thursday	Friday	Saturday	Notes
5_____	6_____	7_____	_____
12_____	13_____	14_____	_____
19_____	20_____	21_____	_____
26_____	27_____	28_____	_____

April 2015

Sunday	Monday	Tuesday	Wednesday
			1_____
5_____	6_____	7_____	8_____
12_____	13_____	14_____	15_____
19_____	20_____	21_____	22_____
26_____	27_____	28_____	29_____

Thursday	Friday	Saturday	Notes
2	3	4	
9	10	11	
16	17	18	
23	24	25	
30			

May 2015

Sunday	Monday	Tuesday	Wednesday
3	4	5	6
10	11	12	13
17	18	19	20
24 / 31	25	26	27

Thursday	Friday	Saturday	Notes
_____	1_____	2_____	_____
7_____	8_____	9_____	
14_____	15_____	16_____	
21_____	22_____	23_____	
28_____	29_____	30_____	

June 2015

Sunday	Monday	Tuesday	Wednesday
	1	2	3
7	8	9	10
14	15	16	17
21	22	23	24
28	29	30	

Thursday	Friday	Saturday	Notes
4 _____	5 _____	6 _____	_____
11 _____	12 _____	13 _____	_____
18 _____	19 _____	20 _____	_____
25 _____	26 _____	27 _____	_____
			_____

July 2015

Sunday	Monday	Tuesday	Wednesday
			1
5	6	7	8
12	13	14	15
19	20	21	22
26	27	28	29

Thursday	Friday	Saturday	Notes
2_____	3_____	4_____	_____
9_____	10_____	11_____	_____
16_____	17_____	18_____	_____
23_____	24_____	25_____	_____
30_____	31_____		_____

August 2015

Sunday	Monday	Tuesday	Wednesday
2	3	4	5
9	10	11	12
16	17	18	19
23 30	24 31	25	26

Thursday	Friday	Saturday	Notes
		1_____	
6_____	7_____	8_____	
13_____	14_____	15_____	
20_____	21_____	22_____	
27_____	28_____	29_____	

September 2015

Sunday	Monday	Tuesday	Wednesday
		1	2
6	7	8	9
13	14	15	16
20	21	22	23
27	28	29	30

Thursday	Friday	Saturday	Notes
3_____	4_____	5_____	_____
_____	_____	_____	_____
_____	_____	_____	_____
_____	_____	_____	_____
_____	_____	_____	_____
_____	_____	_____	_____
10_____	11_____	12_____	_____
_____	_____	_____	_____
_____	_____	_____	_____
_____	_____	_____	_____
_____	_____	_____	_____
_____	_____	_____	_____
17_____	18_____	19_____	_____
_____	_____	_____	_____
_____	_____	_____	_____
_____	_____	_____	_____
_____	_____	_____	_____
_____	_____	_____	_____
24_____	25_____	26_____	_____
_____	_____	_____	_____
_____	_____	_____	_____
_____	_____	_____	_____
_____	_____	_____	_____
_____	_____	_____	_____
_____	_____	_____	_____
_____	_____	_____	_____
_____	_____	_____	_____
_____	_____	_____	_____
_____	_____	_____	_____

October 2015

Sunday	Monday	Tuesday	Wednesday
4	5	6	7
11	12	13	14
18	19	20	21
25	26	27	28

October 2015

Thursday	Friday	Saturday	Notes
1_____	2_____	3_____	_____
8_____	9_____	10_____	_____
15_____	16_____	17_____	_____
22_____	23_____	24_____	_____
29_____	30_____	31_____	_____

November 2015

Sunday	Monday	Tuesday	Wednesday
1_____	2_____	3_____	4_____
8_____	9_____	10_____	11_____
15_____	16_____	17_____	18_____
22_____	23_____	24_____	25_____
29_____	30_____		

Thursday	Friday	Saturday	Notes
5_____	6_____	7_____	
12_____	13_____	14_____	
19_____	20_____	21_____	
26_____	27_____	28_____	

December 2015

Sunday	Monday	Tuesday	Wednesday
		1	2
6	7	8	9
13	14	15	16
20	21	22	23
27	28	29	30

December 2015

Thursday	Friday	Saturday	Notes
3	4	5	
10	11	12	
17	18	19	
24	25	26	
31			

37

Part Four

Weekly Planner

2015

❖ More writing space for
detailed planning

December 2014

Monday
29

Tuesday
30

Wednesday
31

Thursday
1

Friday
2

Saturday
3

Sunday
4

January 2015

Monday
5

Tuesday
6

Wednesday
7

Thursday
8

Friday
9

Saturday
10

Sunday
11

January 2015

Monday
12_____
_____
_____
_____
_____
_____
_____
_____
_____

Tuesday
13_____
_____
_____
_____
_____
_____
_____
_____
_____

Wednesday
14_____
_____
_____
_____
_____
_____
_____
_____
_____

Thursday
15

Friday
16

Saturday
17

Sunday
18

January 2015

Monday
19

Tuesday
20

Wednesday
21

Thursday

22 _____

_____

_____

_____

_____

_____

_____

_____

_____

Friday

23 _____

_____

_____

_____

_____

_____

_____

_____

_____

Saturday

24 _____

_____

_____

_____

Sunday

25 _____

_____

_____

_____

January 2015

Monday
26_____
_____
_____
_____
_____
_____
_____
_____
_____

Tuesday
27_____
_____
_____
_____
_____
_____
_____
_____
_____

Wednesday
28_____
_____
_____
_____
_____
_____
_____
_____
_____

Thursday

29

Friday

30

Saturday

31

Sunday

1

February 2015

Monday
2

Tuesday
3

Wednesday
4

Thursday
5

Friday
6

Saturday
7

Sunday
8

February 2015

Monday

9 _____
_____
_____
_____
_____
_____
_____
_____
_____

Tuesday

10 _____
_____
_____
_____
_____
_____
_____
_____
_____

Wednesday

11 _____
_____
_____
_____
_____
_____
_____
_____
_____

February 2015

| Thursday |
| 12 |
| |
| |
| |
| |
| |
| |
| |
| |

| Friday |
| 13 |
| |
| |
| |
| |
| |
| |
| |
| |

| Saturday |
| 14 |
| |
| |
| |

| Sunday |
| 15 |
| |
| |
| |

February 2015

Monday
16

Tuesday
17

Wednesday
18

February 2015

Thursday
19

Friday
20

Saturday
21

Sunday
22

February 2015

Monday
23

Tuesday
24

Wednesday
25

Thursday
26
_____
_____
_____
_____
_____
_____
_____
_____
_____

Friday
27
_____
_____
_____
_____
_____
_____
_____
_____
_____

Saturday
28
_____
_____
_____

Sunday
1
_____
_____
_____

March 2015

Monday

2

Tuesday

3

Wednesday

4

Thursday

5

Friday

6

Saturday

7

Sunday

8

March 2015

Monday
9

Tuesday
10

Wednesday
11

Thursday
12

Friday
13

Saturday
14

Sunday
15

March 2015

Monday
16

Tuesday
17

Wednesday
18

Thursday
19

Friday
20

Saturday
21

Sunday
22

March 2015

Monday
23

Tuesday
24

Wednesday
25

Thursday
26

Friday
27

Saturday
28

Sunday
29

March/April 2015

Monday
30

Tuesday
31

Wednesday
1

Thursday
2 _____
_____
_____
_____
_____
_____
_____
_____
_____

Friday
3 _____
_____
_____
_____
_____
_____
_____
_____
_____

Saturday
4 _____
_____
_____
_____

Sunday
5 _____
_____
_____
_____

April 2015

Monday
6

Tuesday
7

Wednesday
8

Thursday

9

Friday

10

Saturday

11

Sunday

12

April 2015

Monday
13

Tuesday
14

Wednesday
15

Thursday
16

Friday
17

Saturday
18

Sunday
19

April 2015

Monday
20

Tuesday
21

Wednesday
22

Thursday
23

Friday
24

Saturday
25

Sunday
26

April 2015

Monday
27

Tuesday
28

Wednesday
29

April/May 2015

Thursday
30

Friday
1

Saturday
2

Sunday
3

May 2015

Monday
4

Tuesday
5

Wednesday
6

Thursday
7

Friday
8

Saturday
9

Sunday
10

May 2015

Monday
11

Tuesday
12

Wednesday
13

Thursday

14

Friday

15

Saturday

16

Sunday

17

May 2015

Monday
18_____
_____
_____
_____
_____
_____
_____
_____
_____

Tuesday
19_____
_____
_____
_____
_____
_____
_____
_____
_____

Wednesday
20_____
_____
_____
_____
_____
_____
_____
_____
_____

Thursday

21

Friday

22

Saturday

23

Sunday

24

May 2015

Monday
25

Tuesday
26

Wednesday
27

Thursday
28

Friday
29

Saturday
30

Sunday
31

June 2015

Monday
1

Tuesday
2

Wednesday
3

Thursday
4

Friday
5

Saturday
6

Sunday
7

June 2015

Monday
8

Tuesday
9

Wednesday
10

June 2015

| Thursday |
| 11 |

| Friday |
| 12 |

| Saturday |
| 13 |

| Sunday |
| 14 |

June 2015

Monday
15

Tuesday
16

Wednesday
17

June 2015

Thursday
18

Friday
19

Saturday
20

Sunday
21

June 2015

Monday
22

Tuesday
23

Wednesday
24

Thursday
25

Friday
26

Saturday
27

Sunday
28

June/July 2015

Monday
29

Tuesday
30

Wednesday
1

Thursday
2

Friday
3

Saturday
4

Sunday
5

July 2015

Monday
6

Tuesday
7

Wednesday
8

Thursday

9

Friday

10

Saturday

11

Sunday

12

July 2015

Monday
13

Tuesday
14

Wednesday
15

Thursday

16

Friday

17

Saturday

18

Sunday

19

July 2015

Monday
20

Tuesday
21

Wednesday
22

July 2015

Thursday
23

Friday
24

Saturday
25

Sunday
26

July 2015

Monday
27

Tuesday
28

Wednesday
29

Thursday

30

Friday

31

Saturday

1

Sunday

2

August 2015

Monday
3

Tuesday
4

Wednesday
5

Thursday

6

Friday

7

Saturday

8

Sunday

9

August 2015

Monday
10

Tuesday
11

Wednesday
12

Thursday
13

Friday
14

Saturday
15

Sunday
16

August 2015

Monday
17_____

Tuesday
18_____

Wednesday
19_____

Thursday
20_____
_____
_____
_____
_____
_____
_____
_____
_____

Friday
21_____
_____
_____
_____
_____
_____
_____
_____
_____

Saturday
22_____
_____
_____
_____

Sunday
23_____
_____
_____
_____

August 2015

Monday
24

Tuesday
25

Wednesday
26

Thursday
27

Friday
28

Saturday
29

Sunday
30

August/September 2015

Monday
31

Tuesday
1

Wednesday
2

| Thursday |
| 3 |

| Friday |
| 4 |

| Saturday |
| 5 |

| Sunday |
| 6 |

September 2015

Monday
7

Tuesday
8

Wednesday
9

September 2015

Thursday
10

Friday
11

Saturday
12

Sunday
13

September 2015

Monday
14

Tuesday
15

Wednesday
16

Thursday
17_____
_____
_____
_____
_____
_____
_____
_____
_____

Friday
18_____
_____
_____
_____
_____
_____
_____
_____
_____

Saturday
19_____
_____
_____
_____

Sunday
20_____
_____
_____
_____

September 2015

Monday
21_____
_____
_____
_____
_____
_____
_____
_____
_____

Tuesday
22_____
_____
_____
_____
_____
_____
_____
_____
_____

Wednesday
23_____
_____
_____
_____
_____
_____
_____
_____
_____

September 2015

Thursday
24

Friday
25

Saturday
26

Sunday
27

September 2015

Monday
28

Tuesday
29

Wednesday
30

Thursday
1

Friday
2

Saturday
3

Sunday
4

October 2015

Monday
5

Tuesday
6

Wednesday
7

Thursday

8 _____
_____
_____
_____
_____
_____
_____
_____
_____

Friday

9 _____
_____
_____
_____
_____
_____
_____
_____
_____

Saturday

10 _____
_____
_____
_____

Sunday

11 _____
_____
_____
_____

October 2015

Monday
12_____
_____
_____
_____
_____
_____
_____
_____
_____

Tuesday
13_____
_____
_____
_____
_____
_____
_____
_____
_____

Wednesday
14_____
_____
_____
_____
_____
_____
_____
_____

Thursday

15

Friday

16

Saturday

17

Sunday

18

October 2015

Monday
19

Tuesday
20

Wednesday
21

Thursday
22

Friday
23

Saturday
24

Sunday
25

October 2015

Monday
26

Tuesday
27

Wednesday
28

Thursday

29_____

_____

_____

_____

_____

_____

_____

_____

_____

Friday

30_____

_____

_____

_____

_____

_____

_____

_____

_____

Saturday

31_____

_____

_____

_____

Sunday

1_____

_____

_____

_____

November 2015

Monday
2

Tuesday
3

Wednesday
4

Thursday
5

Friday
6

Saturday
7

Sunday
8

November 2015

Monday
9

Tuesday
10

Wednesday
11

Thursday
12
_____
_____
_____
_____
_____
_____
_____
_____

Friday
13
_____
_____
_____
_____
_____
_____
_____
_____

Saturday
14
_____
_____
_____

Sunday
15
_____
_____
_____

November 2015

Monday
16

Tuesday
17

Wednesday
18

Thursday
19

Friday
20

Saturday
21

Sunday
22

November 2015

Monday
23

Tuesday
24

Wednesday
25

Thursday
26_____
_____
_____
_____
_____
_____
_____
_____
_____

Friday
27_____
_____
_____
_____
_____
_____
_____
_____
_____

Saturday
28_____
_____
_____
_____

Sunday
29_____
_____
_____
_____

November/December 2015

Monday
30

Tuesday
1

Wednesday
2

Thursday
3 _____
_____
_____
_____
_____
_____
_____
_____
_____

Friday
4 _____
_____
_____
_____
_____
_____
_____
_____
_____

Saturday
5 _____
_____
_____

Sunday
6 _____
_____
_____

December 2015

Monday
7

Tuesday
8

Wednesday
9

Thursday

10 _____

_____

_____

_____

_____

_____

_____

_____

_____

_____

Friday

11 _____

_____

_____

_____

_____

_____

_____

_____

_____

_____

Saturday

12 _____

_____

_____

_____

Sunday

13 _____

_____

_____

_____

December 2015

Monday
14

Tuesday
15

Wednesday
16

Thursday

17

Friday

18

Saturday

19

Sunday

20

December 2015

Monday
21

Tuesday
22

Wednesday
23

Thursday

24_____

_____
_____
_____
_____
_____
_____
_____
_____

Friday

25_____

_____
_____
_____
_____
_____
_____
_____
_____

Saturday

26_____

_____
_____
_____

Sunday

27_____

_____
_____
_____

December 2015

Monday
28

Tuesday
29

Wednesday
30

Thursday

31
_____

_____

_____

_____

_____

_____

_____

_____

_____

Friday

1
_____

_____

_____

_____

_____

_____

_____

_____

_____

Saturday

2
_____

_____

_____

Sunday

3
_____

_____

_____

Part Five
Daily Planner
2015

Great for busy schedules:

- ❖ Time management
- ❖ Appointments
- ❖ Interviews
- ❖ College classes

Daily Plan for Monday, December 29, 2014

12:00	a.m.	
1:00	a.m.	
2:00	a.m.	
3:00	a.m.	
4:00	a.m.	
5:00	a.m.	
6:00	a.m.	
7:00	a.m.	
8:00	a.m.	
9:00	a.m.	
10:00	a.m.	
11:00	a.m.	
12:00	p.m.	
1:00	p.m.	
2:00	p.m.	
3:00	p.m.	
4:00	p.m.	
5:00	p.m.	
6:00	p.m.	
7:00	p.m.	
8:00	p.m.	
9:00	p.m.	
10:00	p.m.	
11:00	p.m.	
12:00	a.m.	

Daily Plan for Tuesday, December 30, 2014

12:00	a.m.	
1:00	a.m.	
2:00	a.m.	
3:00	a.m.	
4:00	a.m.	
5:00	a.m.	
6:00	a.m.	
7:00	a.m.	
8:00	a.m.	
9:00	a.m.	
10:00	a.m.	
11:00	a.m.	
12:00	p.m.	
1:00	p.m.	
2:00	p.m.	
3:00	p.m.	
4:00	p.m.	
5:00	p.m.	
6:00	p.m.	
7:00	p.m.	
8:00	p.m.	
9:00	p.m.	
10:00	p.m.	
11:00	p.m.	
12:00	a.m.	

Daily Plan for Wednesday, December 31, 2014

Time		
12:00	a.m.	
1:00	a.m.	
2:00	a.m.	
3:00	a.m.	
4:00	a.m.	
5:00	a.m.	
6:00	a.m.	
7:00	a.m.	
8:00	a.m.	
9:00	a.m.	
10:00	a.m.	
11:00	a.m.	
12:00	p.m.	
1:00	p.m.	
2:00	p.m.	
3:00	p.m.	
4:00	p.m.	
5:00	p.m.	
6:00	p.m.	
7:00	p.m.	
8:00	p.m.	
9:00	p.m.	
10:00	p.m.	
11:00	p.m.	
12:00	a.m.	

Daily Plan for Thursday, January 1, 2015

Time		
12:00	a.m.	
1:00	a.m.	
2:00	a.m.	
3:00	a.m.	
4:00	a.m.	
5:00	a.m.	
6:00	a.m.	
7:00	a.m.	
8:00	a.m.	
9:00	a.m.	
10:00	a.m.	
11:00	a.m.	
12:00	p.m.	
1:00	p.m.	
2:00	p.m.	
3:00	p.m.	
4:00	p.m.	
5:00	p.m.	
6:00	p.m.	
7:00	p.m.	
8:00	p.m.	
9:00	p.m.	
10:00	p.m.	
11:00	p.m.	
12:00	a.m.	

Daily Plan for Friday, January 2, 2015

Time		
12:00	a.m.	
1:00	a.m.	
2:00	a.m.	
3:00	a.m.	
4:00	a.m.	
5:00	a.m.	
6:00	a.m.	
7:00	a.m.	
8:00	a.m.	
9:00	a.m.	
10:00	a.m.	
11:00	a.m.	
12:00	p.m.	
1:00	p.m.	
2:00	p.m.	
3:00	p.m.	
4:00	p.m.	
5:00	p.m.	
6:00	p.m.	
7:00	p.m.	
8:00	p.m.	
9:00	p.m.	
10:00	p.m.	
11:00	p.m.	
12:00	a.m.	

Daily Plan for Saturday, January 3, 2015

12:00	a.m.	
1:00	a.m.	
2:00	a.m.	
3:00	a.m.	
4:00	a.m.	
5:00	a.m.	
6:00	a.m.	
7:00	a.m.	
8:00	a.m.	
9:00	a.m.	
10:00	a.m.	
11:00	a.m.	
12:00	p.m.	
1:00	p.m.	
2:00	p.m.	
3:00	p.m.	
4:00	p.m.	
5:00	p.m.	
6:00	p.m.	
7:00	p.m.	
8:00	p.m.	
9:00	p.m.	
10:00	p.m.	
11:00	p.m.	
12:00	a.m.	

Daily Plan for Sunday, January 4, 2015

Time	
12:00 a.m.	
1:00 a.m.	
2:00 a.m.	
3:00 a.m.	
4:00 a.m.	
5:00 a.m.	
6:00 a.m.	
7:00 a.m.	
8:00 a.m.	
9:00 a.m.	
10:00 a.m.	
11:00 a.m.	
12:00 p.m.	
1:00 p.m.	
2:00 p.m.	
3:00 p.m.	
4:00 p.m.	
5:00 p.m.	
6:00 p.m.	
7:00 p.m.	
8:00 p.m.	
9:00 p.m.	
10:00 p.m.	
11:00 p.m.	
12:00 a.m.	

Daily Plan for Monday, January 5, 2015

12:00	a.m.	
1:00	a.m.	
2:00	a.m.	
3:00	a.m.	
4:00	a.m.	
5:00	a.m.	
6:00	a.m.	
7:00	a.m.	
8:00	a.m.	
9:00	a.m.	
10:00	a.m.	
11:00	a.m.	
12:00	p.m.	
1:00	p.m.	
2:00	p.m.	
3:00	p.m.	
4:00	p.m.	
5:00	p.m.	
6:00	p.m.	
7:00	p.m.	
8:00	p.m.	
9:00	p.m.	
10:00	p.m.	
11:00	p.m.	
12:00	a.m.	

Daily Plan for Tuesday, January 6, 2015

12:00	a.m.	
1:00	a.m.	
2:00	a.m.	
3:00	a.m.	
4:00	a.m.	
5:00	a.m.	
6:00	a.m.	
7:00	a.m.	
8:00	a.m.	
9:00	a.m.	
10:00	a.m.	
11:00	a.m.	
12:00	p.m.	
1:00	p.m.	
2:00	p.m.	
3:00	p.m.	
4:00	p.m.	
5:00	p.m.	
6:00	p.m.	
7:00	p.m.	
8:00	p.m.	
9:00	p.m.	
10:00	p.m.	
11:00	p.m.	
12:00	a.m.	

Daily Plan for Wednesday, January 7, 2015

12:00	a.m.	
1:00	a.m.	
2:00	a.m.	
3:00	a.m.	
4:00	a.m.	
5:00	a.m.	
6:00	a.m.	
7:00	a.m.	
8:00	a.m.	
9:00	a.m.	
10:00	a.m.	
11:00	a.m.	
12:00	p.m.	
1:00	p.m.	
2:00	p.m.	
3:00	p.m.	
4:00	p.m.	
5:00	p.m.	
6:00	p.m.	
7:00	p.m.	
8:00	p.m.	
9:00	p.m.	
10:00	p.m.	
11:00	p.m.	
12:00	a.m.	

Daily Plan for Thursday, January 8, 2015

12:00	a.m.	
1:00	a.m.	
2:00	a.m.	
3:00	a.m.	
4:00	a.m.	
5:00	a.m.	
6:00	a.m.	
7:00	a.m.	
8:00	a.m.	
9:00	a.m.	
10:00	a.m.	
11:00	a.m.	
12:00	p.m.	
1:00	p.m.	
2:00	p.m.	
3:00	p.m.	
4:00	p.m.	
5:00	p.m.	
6:00	p.m.	
7:00	p.m.	
8:00	p.m.	
9:00	p.m.	
10:00	p.m.	
11:00	p.m.	
12:00	a.m.	

Daily Plan for Friday, January 9, 2015

Time		
12:00	a.m.	
1:00	a.m.	
2:00	a.m.	
3:00	a.m.	
4:00	a.m.	
5:00	a.m.	
6:00	a.m.	
7:00	a.m.	
8:00	a.m.	
9:00	a.m.	
10:00	a.m.	
11:00	a.m.	
12:00	p.m.	
1:00	p.m.	
2:00	p.m.	
3:00	p.m.	
4:00	p.m.	
5:00	p.m.	
6:00	p.m.	
7:00	p.m.	
8:00	p.m.	
9:00	p.m.	
10:00	p.m.	
11:00	p.m.	
12:00	a.m.	

Daily Plan for Saturday, January 10, 2015

12:00	a.m.	
1:00	a.m.	
2:00	a.m.	
3:00	a.m.	
4:00	a.m.	
5:00	a.m.	
6:00	a.m.	
7:00	a.m.	
8:00	a.m.	
9:00	a.m.	
10:00	a.m.	
11:00	a.m.	
12:00	p.m.	
1:00	p.m.	
2:00	p.m.	
3:00	p.m.	
4:00	p.m.	
5:00	p.m.	
6:00	p.m.	
7:00	p.m.	
8:00	p.m.	
9:00	p.m.	
10:00	p.m.	
11:00	p.m.	
12:00	a.m.	

Daily Plan for Sunday, January 11, 2015

12:00	a.m.	
1:00	a.m.	
2:00	a.m.	
3:00	a.m.	
4:00	a.m.	
5:00	a.m.	
6:00	a.m.	
7:00	a.m.	
8:00	a.m.	
9:00	a.m.	
10:00	a.m.	
11:00	a.m.	
12:00	p.m.	
1:00	p.m.	
2:00	p.m.	
3:00	p.m.	
4:00	p.m.	
5:00	p.m.	
6:00	p.m.	
7:00	p.m.	
8:00	p.m.	
9:00	p.m.	
10:00	p.m.	
11:00	p.m.	
12:00	a.m.	

Daily Plan for Monday, January 12, 2015

12:00	a.m.	
1:00	a.m.	
2:00	a.m.	
3:00	a.m.	
4:00	a.m.	
5:00	a.m.	
6:00	a.m.	
7:00	a.m.	
8:00	a.m.	
9:00	a.m.	
10:00	a.m.	
11:00	a.m.	
12:00	p.m.	
1:00	p.m.	
2:00	p.m.	
3:00	p.m.	
4:00	p.m.	
5:00	p.m.	
6:00	p.m.	
7:00	p.m.	
8:00	p.m.	
9:00	p.m.	
10:00	p.m.	
11:00	p.m.	
12:00	a.m.	

Daily Plan for Tuesday, January 13, 2015

12:00	a.m.	
1:00	a.m.	
2:00	a.m.	
3:00	a.m.	
4:00	a.m.	
5:00	a.m.	
6:00	a.m.	
7:00	a.m.	
8:00	a.m.	
9:00	a.m.	
10:00	a.m.	
11:00	a.m.	
12:00	p.m.	
1:00	p.m.	
2:00	p.m.	
3:00	p.m.	
4:00	p.m.	
5:00	p.m.	
6:00	p.m.	
7:00	p.m.	
8:00	p.m.	
9:00	p.m.	
10:00	p.m.	
11:00	p.m.	
12:00	a.m.	

Daily Plan for Wednesday, January 14, 2015

Time		
12:00	a.m.	
1:00	a.m.	
2:00	a.m.	
3:00	a.m.	
4:00	a.m.	
5:00	a.m.	
6:00	a.m.	
7:00	a.m.	
8:00	a.m.	
9:00	a.m.	
10:00	a.m.	
11:00	a.m.	
12:00	p.m.	
1:00	p.m.	
2:00	p.m.	
3:00	p.m.	
4:00	p.m.	
5:00	p.m.	
6:00	p.m.	
7:00	p.m.	
8:00	p.m.	
9:00	p.m.	
10:00	p.m.	
11:00	p.m.	
12:00	a.m.	

Daily Plan for Thursday, January 15, 2015

12:00	a.m.	
1:00	a.m.	
2:00	a.m.	
3:00	a.m.	
4:00	a.m.	
5:00	a.m.	
6:00	a.m.	
7:00	a.m.	
8:00	a.m.	
9:00	a.m.	
10:00	a.m.	
11:00	a.m.	
12:00	p.m.	
1:00	p.m.	
2:00	p.m.	
3:00	p.m.	
4:00	p.m.	
5:00	p.m.	
6:00	p.m.	
7:00	p.m.	
8:00	p.m.	
9:00	p.m.	
10:00	p.m.	
11:00	p.m.	
12:00	a.m.	

Daily Plan for Friday, January 16, 2015

12:00	a.m.	
1:00	a.m.	
2:00	a.m.	
3:00	a.m.	
4:00	a.m.	
5:00	a.m.	
6:00	a.m.	
7:00	a.m.	
8:00	a.m.	
9:00	a.m.	
10:00	a.m.	
11:00	a.m.	
12:00	p.m.	
1:00	p.m.	
2:00	p.m.	
3:00	p.m.	
4:00	p.m.	
5:00	p.m.	
6:00	p.m.	
7:00	p.m.	
8:00	p.m.	
9:00	p.m.	
10:00	p.m.	
11:00	p.m.	
12:00	a.m.	

Daily Plan for Saturday, January 17, 2015

12:00	a.m.	
1:00	a.m.	
2:00	a.m.	
3:00	a.m.	
4:00	a.m.	
5:00	a.m.	
6:00	a.m.	
7:00	a.m.	
8:00	a.m.	
9:00	a.m.	
10:00	a.m.	
11:00	a.m.	
12:00	p.m.	
1:00	p.m.	
2:00	p.m.	
3:00	p.m.	
4:00	p.m.	
5:00	p.m.	
6:00	p.m.	
7:00	p.m.	
8:00	p.m.	
9:00	p.m.	
10:00	p.m.	
11:00	p.m.	
12:00	a.m.	

Daily Plan for Sunday, January 18, 2015

12:00	a.m.	
1:00	a.m.	
2:00	a.m.	
3:00	a.m.	
4:00	a.m.	
5:00	a.m.	
6:00	a.m.	
7:00	a.m.	
8:00	a.m.	
9:00	a.m.	
10:00	a.m.	
11:00	a.m.	
12:00	p.m.	
1:00	p.m.	
2:00	p.m.	
3:00	p.m.	
4:00	p.m.	
5:00	p.m.	
6:00	p.m.	
7:00	p.m.	
8:00	p.m.	
9:00	p.m.	
10:00	p.m.	
11:00	p.m.	
12:00	a.m.	

Daily Plan for Monday, January 19, 2015

12:00	a.m.	
1:00	a.m.	
2:00	a.m.	
3:00	a.m.	
4:00	a.m.	
5:00	a.m.	
6:00	a.m.	
7:00	a.m.	
8:00	a.m.	
9:00	a.m.	
10:00	a.m.	
11:00	a.m.	
12:00	p.m.	
1:00	p.m.	
2:00	p.m.	
3:00	p.m.	
4:00	p.m.	
5:00	p.m.	
6:00	p.m.	
7:00	p.m.	
8:00	p.m.	
9:00	p.m.	
10:00	p.m.	
11:00	p.m.	
12:00	a.m.	

Daily Plan for Tuesday, January 20, 2015

12:00	a.m.	
1:00	a.m.	
2:00	a.m.	
3:00	a.m.	
4:00	a.m.	
5:00	a.m.	
6:00	a.m.	
7:00	a.m.	
8:00	a.m.	
9:00	a.m.	
10:00	a.m.	
11:00	a.m.	
12:00	p.m.	
1:00	p.m.	
2:00	p.m.	
3:00	p.m.	
4:00	p.m.	
5:00	p.m.	
6:00	p.m.	
7:00	p.m.	
8:00	p.m.	
9:00	p.m.	
10:00	p.m.	
11:00	p.m.	
12:00	a.m.	

Daily Plan for Wednesday, January 21, 2015

Time		
12:00	a.m.	
1:00	a.m.	
2:00	a.m.	
3:00	a.m.	
4:00	a.m.	
5:00	a.m.	
6:00	a.m.	
7:00	a.m.	
8:00	a.m.	
9:00	a.m.	
10:00	a.m.	
11:00	a.m.	
12:00	p.m.	
1:00	p.m.	
2:00	p.m.	
3:00	p.m.	
4:00	p.m.	
5:00	p.m.	
6:00	p.m.	
7:00	p.m.	
8:00	p.m.	
9:00	p.m.	
10:00	p.m.	
11:00	p.m.	
12:00	a.m.	

Daily Plan for Thursday, January 22, 2015

12:00	a.m.	
1:00	a.m.	
2:00	a.m.	
3:00	a.m.	
4:00	a.m.	
5:00	a.m.	
6:00	a.m.	
7:00	a.m.	
8:00	a.m.	
9:00	a.m.	
10:00	a.m.	
11:00	a.m.	
12:00	p.m.	
1:00	p.m.	
2:00	p.m.	
3:00	p.m.	
4:00	p.m.	
5:00	p.m.	
6:00	p.m.	
7:00	p.m.	
8:00	p.m.	
9:00	p.m.	
10:00	p.m.	
11:00	p.m.	
12:00	a.m.	

Daily Plan for Friday, January 23, 2015

12:00	a.m.	
1:00	a.m.	
2:00	a.m.	
3:00	a.m.	
4:00	a.m.	
5:00	a.m.	
6:00	a.m.	
7:00	a.m.	
8:00	a.m.	
9:00	a.m.	
10:00	a.m.	
11:00	a.m.	
12:00	p.m.	
1:00	p.m.	
2:00	p.m.	
3:00	p.m.	
4:00	p.m.	
5:00	p.m.	
6:00	p.m.	
7:00	p.m.	
8:00	p.m.	
9:00	p.m.	
10:00	p.m.	
11:00	p.m.	
12:00	a.m.	

Daily Plan for Saturday, January 24, 2015

12:00	a.m.	
1:00	a.m.	
2:00	a.m.	
3:00	a.m.	
4:00	a.m.	
5:00	a.m.	
6:00	a.m.	
7:00	a.m.	
8:00	a.m.	
9:00	a.m.	
10:00	a.m.	
11:00	a.m.	
12:00	p.m.	
1:00	p.m.	
2:00	p.m.	
3:00	p.m.	
4:00	p.m.	
5:00	p.m.	
6:00	p.m.	
7:00	p.m.	
8:00	p.m.	
9:00	p.m.	
10:00	p.m.	
11:00	p.m.	
12:00	a.m.	

Daily Plan for Sunday, January 25, 2015

12:00	a.m.	
1:00	a.m.	
2:00	a.m.	
3:00	a.m.	
4:00	a.m.	
5:00	a.m.	
6:00	a.m.	
7:00	a.m.	
8:00	a.m.	
9:00	a.m.	
10:00	a.m.	
11:00	a.m.	
12:00	p.m.	
1:00	p.m.	
2:00	p.m.	
3:00	p.m.	
4:00	p.m.	
5:00	p.m.	
6:00	p.m.	
7:00	p.m.	
8:00	p.m.	
9:00	p.m.	
10:00	p.m.	
11:00	p.m.	
12:00	a.m.	

Daily Plan for Monday, January 26, 2015

12:00	a.m.	
1:00	a.m.	
2:00	a.m.	
3:00	a.m.	
4:00	a.m.	
5:00	a.m.	
6:00	a.m.	
7:00	a.m.	
8:00	a.m.	
9:00	a.m.	
10:00	a.m.	
11:00	a.m.	
12:00	p.m.	
1:00	p.m.	
2:00	p.m.	
3:00	p.m.	
4:00	p.m.	
5:00	p.m.	
6:00	p.m.	
7:00	p.m.	
8:00	p.m.	
9:00	p.m.	
10:00	p.m.	
11:00	p.m.	
12:00	a.m.	

Daily Plan for Tuesday, January 27, 2015

12:00	a.m.	
1:00	a.m.	
2:00	a.m.	
3:00	a.m.	
4:00	a.m.	
5:00	a.m.	
6:00	a.m.	
7:00	a.m.	
8:00	a.m.	
9:00	a.m.	
10:00	a.m.	
11:00	a.m.	
12:00	p.m.	
1:00	p.m.	
2:00	p.m.	
3:00	p.m.	
4:00	p.m.	
5:00	p.m.	
6:00	p.m.	
7:00	p.m.	
8:00	p.m.	
9:00	p.m.	
10:00	p.m.	
11:00	p.m.	
12:00	a.m.	

Daily Plan for Wednesday, January 28, 2015

12:00	a.m.	
1:00	a.m.	
2:00	a.m.	
3:00	a.m.	
4:00	a.m.	
5:00	a.m.	
6:00	a.m.	
7:00	a.m.	
8:00	a.m.	
9:00	a.m.	
10:00	a.m.	
11:00	a.m.	
12:00	p.m.	
1:00	p.m.	
2:00	p.m.	
3:00	p.m.	
4:00	p.m.	
5:00	p.m.	
6:00	p.m.	
7:00	p.m.	
8:00	p.m.	
9:00	p.m.	
10:00	p.m.	
11:00	p.m.	
12:00	a.m.	

Daily Plan for Thursday, January 29, 2015

12:00	a.m.	
1:00	a.m.	
2:00	a.m.	
3:00	a.m.	
4:00	a.m.	
5:00	a.m.	
6:00	a.m.	
7:00	a.m.	
8:00	a.m.	
9:00	a.m.	
10:00	a.m.	
11:00	a.m.	
12:00	p.m.	
1:00	p.m.	
2:00	p.m.	
3:00	p.m.	
4:00	p.m.	
5:00	p.m.	
6:00	p.m.	
7:00	p.m.	
8:00	p.m.	
9:00	p.m.	
10:00	p.m.	
11:00	p.m.	
12:00	a.m.	

Daily Plan for Friday, January 30, 2015

12:00	a.m.	
1:00	a.m.	
2:00	a.m.	
3:00	a.m.	
4:00	a.m.	
5:00	a.m.	
6:00	a.m.	
7:00	a.m.	
8:00	a.m.	
9:00	a.m.	
10:00	a.m.	
11:00	a.m.	
12:00	p.m.	
1:00	p.m.	
2:00	p.m.	
3:00	p.m.	
4:00	p.m.	
5:00	p.m.	
6:00	p.m.	
7:00	p.m.	
8:00	p.m.	
9:00	p.m.	
10:00	p.m.	
11:00	p.m.	
12:00	a.m.	

Daily Plan for Saturday, January 31, 2015

12:00	a.m.	
1:00	a.m.	
2:00	a.m.	
3:00	a.m.	
4:00	a.m.	
5:00	a.m.	
6:00	a.m.	
7:00	a.m.	
8:00	a.m.	
9:00	a.m.	
10:00	a.m.	
11:00	a.m.	
12:00	p.m.	
1:00	p.m.	
2:00	p.m.	
3:00	p.m.	
4:00	p.m.	
5:00	p.m.	
6:00	p.m.	
7:00	p.m.	
8:00	p.m.	
9:00	p.m.	
10:00	p.m.	
11:00	p.m.	
12:00	a.m.	

Daily Plan for Sunday, February 1, 2015

12:00	a.m.	
1:00	a.m.	
2:00	a.m.	
3:00	a.m.	
4:00	a.m.	
5:00	a.m.	
6:00	a.m.	
7:00	a.m.	
8:00	a.m.	
9:00	a.m.	
10:00	a.m.	
11:00	a.m.	
12:00	p.m.	
1:00	p.m.	
2:00	p.m.	
3:00	p.m.	
4:00	p.m.	
5:00	p.m.	
6:00	p.m.	
7:00	p.m.	
8:00	p.m.	
9:00	p.m.	
10:00	p.m.	
11:00	p.m.	
12:00	a.m.	

Daily Plan for Monday, February 2, 2015

12:00	a.m.	
1:00	a.m.	
2:00	a.m.	
3:00	a.m.	
4:00	a.m.	
5:00	a.m.	
6:00	a.m.	
7:00	a.m.	
8:00	a.m.	
9:00	a.m.	
10:00	a.m.	
11:00	a.m.	
12:00	p.m.	
1:00	p.m.	
2:00	p.m.	
3:00	p.m.	
4:00	p.m.	
5:00	p.m.	
6:00	p.m.	
7:00	p.m.	
8:00	p.m.	
9:00	p.m.	
10:00	p.m.	
11:00	p.m.	
12:00	a.m.	

Daily Plan for Tuesday, February 3, 2015

12:00	a.m.	
1:00	a.m.	
2:00	a.m.	
3:00	a.m.	
4:00	a.m.	
5:00	a.m.	
6:00	a.m.	
7:00	a.m.	
8:00	a.m.	
9:00	a.m.	
10:00	a.m.	
11:00	a.m.	
12:00	p.m.	
1:00	p.m.	
2:00	p.m.	
3:00	p.m.	
4:00	p.m.	
5:00	p.m.	
6:00	p.m.	
7:00	p.m.	
8:00	p.m.	
9:00	p.m.	
10:00	p.m.	
11:00	p.m.	
12:00	a.m.	

Daily Plan for Wednesday, February 4, 2015

12:00	a.m.	
1:00	a.m.	
2:00	a.m.	
3:00	a.m.	
4:00	a.m.	
5:00	a.m.	
6:00	a.m.	
7:00	a.m.	
8:00	a.m.	
9:00	a.m.	
10:00	a.m.	
11:00	a.m.	
12:00	p.m.	
1:00	p.m.	
2:00	p.m.	
3:00	p.m.	
4:00	p.m.	
5:00	p.m.	
6:00	p.m.	
7:00	p.m.	
8:00	p.m.	
9:00	p.m.	
10:00	p.m.	
11:00	p.m.	
12:00	a.m.	

Daily Plan for Thursday, February 5, 2015

12:00	a.m.	
1:00	a.m.	
2:00	a.m.	
3:00	a.m.	
4:00	a.m.	
5:00	a.m.	
6:00	a.m.	
7:00	a.m.	
8:00	a.m.	
9:00	a.m.	
10:00	a.m.	
11:00	a.m.	
12:00	p.m.	
1:00	p.m.	
2:00	p.m.	
3:00	p.m.	
4:00	p.m.	
5:00	p.m.	
6:00	p.m.	
7:00	p.m.	
8:00	p.m.	
9:00	p.m.	
10:00	p.m.	
11:00	p.m.	
12:00	a.m.	

Daily Plan for Friday, February 6, 2015

12:00	a.m.	
1:00	a.m.	
2:00	a.m.	
3:00	a.m.	
4:00	a.m.	
5:00	a.m.	
6:00	a.m.	
7:00	a.m.	
8:00	a.m.	
9:00	a.m.	
10:00	a.m.	
11:00	a.m.	
12:00	p.m.	
1:00	p.m.	
2:00	p.m.	
3:00	p.m.	
4:00	p.m.	
5:00	p.m.	
6:00	p.m.	
7:00	p.m.	
8:00	p.m.	
9:00	p.m.	
10:00	p.m.	
11:00	p.m.	
12:00	a.m.	

Daily Plan for Saturday, February 7, 2015

Time	
12:00 a.m.	
1:00 a.m.	
2:00 a.m.	
3:00 a.m.	
4:00 a.m.	
5:00 a.m.	
6:00 a.m.	
7:00 a.m.	
8:00 a.m.	
9:00 a.m.	
10:00 a.m.	
11:00 a.m.	
12:00 p.m.	
1:00 p.m.	
2:00 p.m.	
3:00 p.m.	
4:00 p.m.	
5:00 p.m.	
6:00 p.m.	
7:00 p.m.	
8:00 p.m.	
9:00 p.m.	
10:00 p.m.	
11:00 p.m.	
12:00 a.m.	

Daily Plan for Sunday, February 8, 2015

Time		
12:00	a.m.	
1:00	a.m.	
2:00	a.m.	
3:00	a.m.	
4:00	a.m.	
5:00	a.m.	
6:00	a.m.	
7:00	a.m.	
8:00	a.m.	
9:00	a.m.	
10:00	a.m.	
11:00	a.m.	
12:00	p.m.	
1:00	p.m.	
2:00	p.m.	
3:00	p.m.	
4:00	p.m.	
5:00	p.m.	
6:00	p.m.	
7:00	p.m.	
8:00	p.m.	
9:00	p.m.	
10:00	p.m.	
11:00	p.m.	
12:00	a.m.	

Daily Plan for Monday, February 9, 2015

12:00	a.m.	
1:00	a.m.	
2:00	a.m.	
3:00	a.m.	
4:00	a.m.	
5:00	a.m.	
6:00	a.m.	
7:00	a.m.	
8:00	a.m.	
9:00	a.m.	
10:00	a.m.	
11:00	a.m.	
12:00	p.m.	
1:00	p.m.	
2:00	p.m.	
3:00	p.m.	
4:00	p.m.	
5:00	p.m.	
6:00	p.m.	
7:00	p.m.	
8:00	p.m.	
9:00	p.m.	
10:00	p.m.	
11:00	p.m.	
12:00	a.m.	

Daily Plan for Tuesday, February 10, 2015

12:00	a.m.	
1:00	a.m.	
2:00	a.m.	
3:00	a.m.	
4:00	a.m.	
5:00	a.m.	
6:00	a.m.	
7:00	a.m.	
8:00	a.m.	
9:00	a.m.	
10:00	a.m.	
11:00	a.m.	
12:00	p.m.	
1:00	p.m.	
2:00	p.m.	
3:00	p.m.	
4:00	p.m.	
5:00	p.m.	
6:00	p.m.	
7:00	p.m.	
8:00	p.m.	
9:00	p.m.	
10:00	p.m.	
11:00	p.m.	
12:00	a.m.	

Daily Plan for Wednesday, February 11, 2015

12:00	a.m.	
1:00	a.m.	
2:00	a.m.	
3:00	a.m.	
4:00	a.m.	
5:00	a.m.	
6:00	a.m.	
7:00	a.m.	
8:00	a.m.	
9:00	a.m.	
10:00	a.m.	
11:00	a.m.	
12:00	p.m.	
1:00	p.m.	
2:00	p.m.	
3:00	p.m.	
4:00	p.m.	
5:00	p.m.	
6:00	p.m.	
7:00	p.m.	
8:00	p.m.	
9:00	p.m.	
10:00	p.m.	
11:00	p.m.	
12:00	a.m.	

Daily Plan for Thursday, February 12, 2015

12:00	a.m.	
1:00	a.m.	
2:00	a.m.	
3:00	a.m.	
4:00	a.m.	
5:00	a.m.	
6:00	a.m.	
7:00	a.m.	
8:00	a.m.	
9:00	a.m.	
10:00	a.m.	
11:00	a.m.	
12:00	p.m.	
1:00	p.m.	
2:00	p.m.	
3:00	p.m.	
4:00	p.m.	
5:00	p.m.	
6:00	p.m.	
7:00	p.m.	
8:00	p.m.	
9:00	p.m.	
10:00	p.m.	
11:00	p.m.	
12:00	a.m.	

Daily Plan for Friday, February 13, 2015

12:00	a.m.	
1:00	a.m.	
2:00	a.m.	
3:00	a.m.	
4:00	a.m.	
5:00	a.m.	
6:00	a.m.	
7:00	a.m.	
8:00	a.m.	
9:00	a.m.	
10:00	a.m.	
11:00	a.m.	
12:00	p.m.	
1:00	p.m.	
2:00	p.m.	
3:00	p.m.	
4:00	p.m.	
5:00	p.m.	
6:00	p.m.	
7:00	p.m.	
8:00	p.m.	
9:00	p.m.	
10:00	p.m.	
11:00	p.m.	
12:00	a.m.	

Daily Plan for Saturday, February 14, 2015

12:00	a.m.	
1:00	a.m.	
2:00	a.m.	
3:00	a.m.	
4:00	a.m.	
5:00	a.m.	
6:00	a.m.	
7:00	a.m.	
8:00	a.m.	
9:00	a.m.	
10:00	a.m.	
11:00	a.m.	
12:00	p.m.	
1:00	p.m.	
2:00	p.m.	
3:00	p.m.	
4:00	p.m.	
5:00	p.m.	
6:00	p.m.	
7:00	p.m.	
8:00	p.m.	
9:00	p.m.	
10:00	p.m.	
11:00	p.m.	
12:00	a.m.	

Daily Plan for Sunday, February 15, 2015

12:00	a.m.	
1:00	a.m.	
2:00	a.m.	
3:00	a.m.	
4:00	a.m.	
5:00	a.m.	
6:00	a.m.	
7:00	a.m.	
8:00	a.m.	
9:00	a.m.	
10:00	a.m.	
11:00	a.m.	
12:00	p.m.	
1:00	p.m.	
2:00	p.m.	
3:00	p.m.	
4:00	p.m.	
5:00	p.m.	
6:00	p.m.	
7:00	p.m.	
8:00	p.m.	
9:00	p.m.	
10:00	p.m.	
11:00	p.m.	
12:00	a.m.	

Daily Plan for Monday, February 16, 2015

12:00	a.m.	
1:00	a.m.	
2:00	a.m.	
3:00	a.m.	
4:00	a.m.	
5:00	a.m.	
6:00	a.m.	
7:00	a.m.	
8:00	a.m.	
9:00	a.m.	
10:00	a.m.	
11:00	a.m.	
12:00	p.m.	
1:00	p.m.	
2:00	p.m.	
3:00	p.m.	
4:00	p.m.	
5:00	p.m.	
6:00	p.m.	
7:00	p.m.	
8:00	p.m.	
9:00	p.m.	
10:00	p.m.	
11:00	p.m.	
12:00	a.m.	

Daily Plan for Tuesday, February 17, 2015

12:00	a.m.	
1:00	a.m.	
2:00	a.m.	
3:00	a.m.	
4:00	a.m.	
5:00	a.m.	
6:00	a.m.	
7:00	a.m.	
8:00	a.m.	
9:00	a.m.	
10:00	a.m.	
11:00	a.m.	
12:00	p.m.	
1:00	p.m.	
2:00	p.m.	
3:00	p.m.	
4:00	p.m.	
5:00	p.m.	
6:00	p.m.	
7:00	p.m.	
8:00	p.m.	
9:00	p.m.	
10:00	p.m.	
11:00	p.m.	
12:00	a.m.	

Daily Plan for Wednesday, February 18, 2015

12:00	a.m.	
1:00	a.m.	
2:00	a.m.	
3:00	a.m.	
4:00	a.m.	
5:00	a.m.	
6:00	a.m.	
7:00	a.m.	
8:00	a.m.	
9:00	a.m.	
10:00	a.m.	
11:00	a.m.	
12:00	p.m.	
1:00	p.m.	
2:00	p.m.	
3:00	p.m.	
4:00	p.m.	
5:00	p.m.	
6:00	p.m.	
7:00	p.m.	
8:00	p.m.	
9:00	p.m.	
10:00	p.m.	
11:00	p.m.	
12:00	a.m.	

Daily Plan for Thursday, February, 19, 2015

12:00	a.m.	
1:00	a.m.	
2:00	a.m.	
3:00	a.m.	
4:00	a.m.	
5:00	a.m.	
6:00	a.m.	
7:00	a.m.	
8:00	a.m.	
9:00	a.m.	
10:00	a.m.	
11:00	a.m.	
12:00	p.m.	
1:00	p.m.	
2:00	p.m.	
3:00	p.m.	
4:00	p.m.	
5:00	p.m.	
6:00	p.m.	
7:00	p.m.	
8:00	p.m.	
9:00	p.m.	
10:00	p.m.	
11:00	p.m.	
12:00	a.m.	

Daily Plan for Friday, February 20, 2015

12:00	a.m.	
1:00	a.m.	
2:00	a.m.	
3:00	a.m.	
4:00	a.m.	
5:00	a.m.	
6:00	a.m.	
7:00	a.m.	
8:00	a.m.	
9:00	a.m.	
10:00	a.m.	
11:00	a.m.	
12:00	p.m.	
1:00	p.m.	
2:00	p.m.	
3:00	p.m.	
4:00	p.m.	
5:00	p.m.	
6:00	p.m.	
7:00	p.m.	
8:00	p.m.	
9:00	p.m.	
10:00	p.m.	
11:00	p.m.	
12:00	a.m.	

Daily Plan for Saturday, February 21, 2015

Time		
12:00	a.m.	
1:00	a.m.	
2:00	a.m.	
3:00	a.m.	
4:00	a.m.	
5:00	a.m.	
6:00	a.m.	
7:00	a.m.	
8:00	a.m.	
9:00	a.m.	
10:00	a.m.	
11:00	a.m.	
12:00	p.m.	
1:00	p.m.	
2:00	p.m.	
3:00	p.m.	
4:00	p.m.	
5:00	p.m.	
6:00	p.m.	
7:00	p.m.	
8:00	p.m.	
9:00	p.m.	
10:00	p.m.	
11:00	p.m.	
12:00	a.m.	

Daily Plan for Sunday, February 22, 2015

12:00	a.m.	
1:00	a.m.	
2:00	a.m.	
3:00	a.m.	
4:00	a.m.	
5:00	a.m.	
6:00	a.m.	
7:00	a.m.	
8:00	a.m.	
9:00	a.m.	
10:00	a.m.	
11:00	a.m.	
12:00	p.m.	
1:00	p.m.	
2:00	p.m.	
3:00	p.m.	
4:00	p.m.	
5:00	p.m.	
6:00	p.m.	
7:00	p.m.	
8:00	p.m.	
9:00	p.m.	
10:00	p.m.	
11:00	p.m.	
12:00	a.m.	

Daily Plan for Monday, February 23, 2015

12:00	a.m.	
1:00	a.m.	
2:00	a.m.	
3:00	a.m.	
4:00	a.m.	
5:00	a.m.	
6:00	a.m.	
7:00	a.m.	
8:00	a.m.	
9:00	a.m.	
10:00	a.m.	
11:00	a.m.	
12:00	p.m.	
1:00	p.m.	
2:00	p.m.	
3:00	p.m.	
4:00	p.m.	
5:00	p.m.	
6:00	p.m.	
7:00	p.m.	
8:00	p.m.	
9:00	p.m.	
10:00	p.m.	
11:00	p.m.	
12:00	a.m.	

Daily Plan for Tuesday, February 24, 2015

12:00	a.m.	
1:00	a.m.	
2:00	a.m.	
3:00	a.m.	
4:00	a.m.	
5:00	a.m.	
6:00	a.m.	
7:00	a.m.	
8:00	a.m.	
9:00	a.m.	
10:00	a.m.	
11:00	a.m.	
12:00	p.m.	
1:00	p.m.	
2:00	p.m.	
3:00	p.m.	
4:00	p.m.	
5:00	p.m.	
6:00	p.m.	
7:00	p.m.	
8:00	p.m.	
9:00	p.m.	
10:00	p.m.	
11:00	p.m.	
12:00	a.m.	

Daily Plan for Wednesday, February 25, 2015

12:00	a.m.	
1:00	a.m.	
2:00	a.m.	
3:00	a.m.	
4:00	a.m.	
5:00	a.m.	
6:00	a.m.	
7:00	a.m.	
8:00	a.m.	
9:00	a.m.	
10:00	a.m.	
11:00	a.m.	
12:00	p.m.	
1:00	p.m.	
2:00	p.m.	
3:00	p.m.	
4:00	p.m.	
5:00	p.m.	
6:00	p.m.	
7:00	p.m.	
8:00	p.m.	
9:00	p.m.	
10:00	p.m.	
11:00	p.m.	
12:00	a.m.	

Daily Plan for Thursday, February 26, 2015

12:00	a.m.	
1:00	a.m.	
2:00	a.m.	
3:00	a.m.	
4:00	a.m.	
5:00	a.m.	
6:00	a.m.	
7:00	a.m.	
8:00	a.m.	
9:00	a.m.	
10:00	a.m.	
11:00	a.m.	
12:00	p.m.	
1:00	p.m.	
2:00	p.m.	
3:00	p.m.	
4:00	p.m.	
5:00	p.m.	
6:00	p.m.	
7:00	p.m.	
8:00	p.m.	
9:00	p.m.	
10:00	p.m.	
11:00	p.m.	
12:00	a.m.	

Daily Plan for Friday, February 27, 2015

12:00	a.m.	
1:00	a.m.	
2:00	a.m.	
3:00	a.m.	
4:00	a.m.	
5:00	a.m.	
6:00	a.m.	
7:00	a.m.	
8:00	a.m.	
9:00	a.m.	
10:00	a.m.	
11:00	a.m.	
12:00	p.m.	
1:00	p.m.	
2:00	p.m.	
3:00	p.m.	
4:00	p.m.	
5:00	p.m.	
6:00	p.m.	
7:00	p.m.	
8:00	p.m.	
9:00	p.m.	
10:00	p.m.	
11:00	p.m.	
12:00	a.m.	

Daily Plan for Saturday, February 28, 2015

12:00	a.m.	
1:00	a.m.	
2:00	a.m.	
3:00	a.m.	
4:00	a.m.	
5:00	a.m.	
6:00	a.m.	
7:00	a.m.	
8:00	a.m.	
9:00	a.m.	
10:00	a.m.	
11:00	a.m.	
12:00	p.m.	
1:00	p.m.	
2:00	p.m.	
3:00	p.m.	
4:00	p.m.	
5:00	p.m.	
6:00	p.m.	
7:00	p.m.	
8:00	p.m.	
9:00	p.m.	
10:00	p.m.	
11:00	p.m.	
12:00	a.m.	

Daily Plan for Sunday, March 1, 2015

12:00	a.m.	
1:00	a.m.	
2:00	a.m.	
3:00	a.m.	
4:00	a.m.	
5:00	a.m.	
6:00	a.m.	
7:00	a.m.	
8:00	a.m.	
9:00	a.m.	
10:00	a.m.	
11:00	a.m.	
12:00	p.m.	
1:00	p.m.	
2:00	p.m.	
3:00	p.m.	
4:00	p.m.	
5:00	p.m.	
6:00	p.m.	
7:00	p.m.	
8:00	p.m.	
9:00	p.m.	
10:00	p.m.	
11:00	p.m.	
12:00	a.m.	

Daily Plan for Monday, March 2, 2015

12:00	a.m.	
1:00	a.m.	
2:00	a.m.	
3:00	a.m.	
4:00	a.m.	
5:00	a.m.	
6:00	a.m.	
7:00	a.m.	
8:00	a.m.	
9:00	a.m.	
10:00	a.m.	
11:00	a.m.	
12:00	p.m.	
1:00	p.m.	
2:00	p.m.	
3:00	p.m.	
4:00	p.m.	
5:00	p.m.	
6:00	p.m.	
7:00	p.m.	
8:00	p.m.	
9:00	p.m.	
10:00	p.m.	
11:00	p.m.	
12:00	a.m.	

Daily Plan for Tuesday, March 3, 2015

12:00	a.m.	
1:00	a.m.	
2:00	a.m.	
3:00	a.m.	
4:00	a.m.	
5:00	a.m.	
6:00	a.m.	
7:00	a.m.	
8:00	a.m.	
9:00	a.m.	
10:00	a.m.	
11:00	a.m.	
12:00	p.m.	
1:00	p.m.	
2:00	p.m.	
3:00	p.m.	
4:00	p.m.	
5:00	p.m.	
6:00	p.m.	
7:00	p.m.	
8:00	p.m.	
9:00	p.m.	
10:00	p.m.	
11:00	p.m.	
12:00	a.m.	

Daily Plan for Wednesday, March 4, 2015

12:00	a.m.	
1:00	a.m.	
2:00	a.m.	
3:00	a.m.	
4:00	a.m.	
5:00	a.m.	
6:00	a.m.	
7:00	a.m.	
8:00	a.m.	
9:00	a.m.	
10:00	a.m.	
11:00	a.m.	
12:00	p.m.	
1:00	p.m.	
2:00	p.m.	
3:00	p.m.	
4:00	p.m.	
5:00	p.m.	
6:00	p.m.	
7:00	p.m.	
8:00	p.m.	
9:00	p.m.	
10:00	p.m.	
11:00	p.m.	
12:00	a.m.	

Daily Plan for Thursday, March 5, 2015

Time	
12:00 a.m.	
1:00 a.m.	
2:00 a.m.	
3:00 a.m.	
4:00 a.m.	
5:00 a.m.	
6:00 a.m.	
7:00 a.m.	
8:00 a.m.	
9:00 a.m.	
10:00 a.m.	
11:00 a.m.	
12:00 p.m.	
1:00 p.m.	
2:00 p.m.	
3:00 p.m.	
4:00 p.m.	
5:00 p.m.	
6:00 p.m.	
7:00 p.m.	
8:00 p.m.	
9:00 p.m.	
10:00 p.m.	
11:00 p.m.	
12:00 a.m.	

Daily Plan for Friday, March 6, 2015

12:00	a.m.	
1:00	a.m.	
2:00	a.m.	
3:00	a.m.	
4:00	a.m.	
5:00	a.m.	
6:00	a.m.	
7:00	a.m.	
8:00	a.m.	
9:00	a.m.	
10:00	a.m.	
11:00	a.m.	
12:00	p.m.	
1:00	p.m.	
2:00	p.m.	
3:00	p.m.	
4:00	p.m.	
5:00	p.m.	
6:00	p.m.	
7:00	p.m.	
8:00	p.m.	
9:00	p.m.	
10:00	p.m.	
11:00	p.m.	
12:00	a.m.	

Daily Plan for Saturday, March 7, 2015

12:00	a.m.	
1:00	a.m.	
2:00	a.m.	
3:00	a.m.	
4:00	a.m.	
5:00	a.m.	
6:00	a.m.	
7:00	a.m.	
8:00	a.m.	
9:00	a.m.	
10:00	a.m.	
11:00	a.m.	
12:00	p.m.	
1:00	p.m.	
2:00	p.m.	
3:00	p.m.	
4:00	p.m.	
5:00	p.m.	
6:00	p.m.	
7:00	p.m.	
8:00	p.m.	
9:00	p.m.	
10:00	p.m.	
11:00	p.m.	
12:00	a.m.	

Daily Plan for Sunday, March 8, 2015

12:00	a.m.	
1:00	a.m.	
2:00	a.m.	
3:00	a.m.	
4:00	a.m.	
5:00	a.m.	
6:00	a.m.	
7:00	a.m.	
8:00	a.m.	
9:00	a.m.	
10:00	a.m.	
11:00	a.m.	
12:00	p.m.	
1:00	p.m.	
2:00	p.m.	
3:00	p.m.	
4:00	p.m.	
5:00	p.m.	
6:00	p.m.	
7:00	p.m.	
8:00	p.m.	
9:00	p.m.	
10:00	p.m.	
11:00	p.m.	
12:00	a.m.	

Daily Plan for Monday, March 9, 2015

12:00	a.m.	
1:00	a.m.	
2:00	a.m.	
3:00	a.m.	
4:00	a.m.	
5:00	a.m.	
6:00	a.m.	
7:00	a.m.	
8:00	a.m.	
9:00	a.m.	
10:00	a.m.	
11:00	a.m.	
12:00	p.m.	
1:00	p.m.	
2:00	p.m.	
3:00	p.m.	
4:00	p.m.	
5:00	p.m.	
6:00	p.m.	
7:00	p.m.	
8:00	p.m.	
9:00	p.m.	
10:00	p.m.	
11:00	p.m.	
12:00	a.m.	

Daily Plan for Tuesday, March 10, 2015

12:00	a.m.	
1:00	a.m.	
2:00	a.m.	
3:00	a.m.	
4:00	a.m.	
5:00	a.m.	
6:00	a.m.	
7:00	a.m.	
8:00	a.m.	
9:00	a.m.	
10:00	a.m.	
11:00	a.m.	
12:00	p.m.	
1:00	p.m.	
2:00	p.m.	
3:00	p.m.	
4:00	p.m.	
5:00	p.m.	
6:00	p.m.	
7:00	p.m.	
8:00	p.m.	
9:00	p.m.	
10:00	p.m.	
11:00	p.m.	
12:00	a.m.	

Daily Plan for Wednesday, March 11, 2015

12:00	a.m.	
1:00	a.m.	
2:00	a.m.	
3:00	a.m.	
4:00	a.m.	
5:00	a.m.	
6:00	a.m.	
7:00	a.m.	
8:00	a.m.	
9:00	a.m.	
10:00	a.m.	
11:00	a.m.	
12:00	p.m.	
1:00	p.m.	
2:00	p.m.	
3:00	p.m.	
4:00	p.m.	
5:00	p.m.	
6:00	p.m.	
7:00	p.m.	
8:00	p.m.	
9:00	p.m.	
10:00	p.m.	
11:00	p.m.	
12:00	a.m.	

Daily Plan for Thursday, March 12, 2015

12:00	a.m.	
1:00	a.m.	
2:00	a.m.	
3:00	a.m.	
4:00	a.m.	
5:00	a.m.	
6:00	a.m.	
7:00	a.m.	
8:00	a.m.	
9:00	a.m.	
10:00	a.m.	
11:00	a.m.	
12:00	p.m.	
1:00	p.m.	
2:00	p.m.	
3:00	p.m.	
4:00	p.m.	
5:00	p.m.	
6:00	p.m.	
7:00	p.m.	
8:00	p.m.	
9:00	p.m.	
10:00	p.m.	
11:00	p.m.	
12:00	a.m.	

Daily Plan for Friday, March 13, 2015

12:00	a.m.	
1:00	a.m.	
2:00	a.m.	
3:00	a.m.	
4:00	a.m.	
5:00	a.m.	
6:00	a.m.	
7:00	a.m.	
8:00	a.m.	
9:00	a.m.	
10:00	a.m.	
11:00	a.m.	
12:00	p.m.	
1:00	p.m.	
2:00	p.m.	
3:00	p.m.	
4:00	p.m.	
5:00	p.m.	
6:00	p.m.	
7:00	p.m.	
8:00	p.m.	
9:00	p.m.	
10:00	p.m.	
11:00	p.m.	
12:00	a.m.	

Daily Plan for Saturday, March 14, 2015

Time	
12:00 a.m.	
1:00 a.m.	
2:00 a.m.	
3:00 a.m.	
4:00 a.m.	
5:00 a.m.	
6:00 a.m.	
7:00 a.m.	
8:00 a.m.	
9:00 a.m.	
10:00 a.m.	
11:00 a.m.	
12:00 p.m.	
1:00 p.m.	
2:00 p.m.	
3:00 p.m.	
4:00 p.m.	
5:00 p.m.	
6:00 p.m.	
7:00 p.m.	
8:00 p.m.	
9:00 p.m.	
10:00 p.m.	
11:00 p.m.	
12:00 a.m.	

Daily Plan for Sunday, March 15, 2015

12:00	a.m.	
1:00	a.m.	
2:00	a.m.	
3:00	a.m.	
4:00	a.m.	
5:00	a.m.	
6:00	a.m.	
7:00	a.m.	
8:00	a.m.	
9:00	a.m.	
10:00	a.m.	
11:00	a.m.	
12:00	p.m.	
1:00	p.m.	
2:00	p.m.	
3:00	p.m.	
4:00	p.m.	
5:00	p.m.	
6:00	p.m.	
7:00	p.m.	
8:00	p.m.	
9:00	p.m.	
10:00	p.m.	
11:00	p.m.	
12:00	a.m.	

Daily Plan for Monday, March 16, 2015

12:00	a.m.	
1:00	a.m.	
2:00	a.m.	
3:00	a.m.	
4:00	a.m.	
5:00	a.m.	
6:00	a.m.	
7:00	a.m.	
8:00	a.m.	
9:00	a.m.	
10:00	a.m.	
11:00	a.m.	
12:00	p.m.	
1:00	p.m.	
2:00	p.m.	
3:00	p.m.	
4:00	p.m.	
5:00	p.m.	
6:00	p.m.	
7:00	p.m.	
8:00	p.m.	
9:00	p.m.	
10:00	p.m.	
11:00	p.m.	
12:00	a.m.	

Daily Plan for Tuesday, March 17, 2015

12:00	a.m.	
1:00	a.m.	
2:00	a.m.	
3:00	a.m.	
4:00	a.m.	
5:00	a.m.	
6:00	a.m.	
7:00	a.m.	
8:00	a.m.	
9:00	a.m.	
10:00	a.m.	
11:00	a.m.	
12:00	p.m.	
1:00	p.m.	
2:00	p.m.	
3:00	p.m.	
4:00	p.m.	
5:00	p.m.	
6:00	p.m.	
7:00	p.m.	
8:00	p.m.	
9:00	p.m.	
10:00	p.m.	
11:00	p.m.	
12:00	a.m.	

Daily Plan for Wednesday, March 18, 2015

12:00	a.m.	
1:00	a.m.	
2:00	a.m.	
3:00	a.m.	
4:00	a.m.	
5:00	a.m.	
6:00	a.m.	
7:00	a.m.	
8:00	a.m.	
9:00	a.m.	
10:00	a.m.	
11:00	a.m.	
12:00	p.m.	
1:00	p.m.	
2:00	p.m.	
3:00	p.m.	
4:00	p.m.	
5:00	p.m.	
6:00	p.m.	
7:00	p.m.	
8:00	p.m.	
9:00	p.m.	
10:00	p.m.	
11:00	p.m.	
12:00	a.m.	

Daily Plan for Thursday, March 19, 2015

12:00	a.m.	
1:00	a.m.	
2:00	a.m.	
3:00	a.m.	
4:00	a.m.	
5:00	a.m.	
6:00	a.m.	
7:00	a.m.	
8:00	a.m.	
9:00	a.m.	
10:00	a.m.	
11:00	a.m.	
12:00	p.m.	
1:00	p.m.	
2:00	p.m.	
3:00	p.m.	
4:00	p.m.	
5:00	p.m.	
6:00	p.m.	
7:00	p.m.	
8:00	p.m.	
9:00	p.m.	
10:00	p.m.	
11:00	p.m.	
12:00	a.m.	

Daily Plan for Friday, March 20, 2015

12:00	a.m.	
1:00	a.m.	
2:00	a.m.	
3:00	a.m.	
4:00	a.m.	
5:00	a.m.	
6:00	a.m.	
7:00	a.m.	
8:00	a.m.	
9:00	a.m.	
10:00	a.m.	
11:00	a.m.	
12:00	p.m.	
1:00	p.m.	
2:00	p.m.	
3:00	p.m.	
4:00	p.m.	
5:00	p.m.	
6:00	p.m.	
7:00	p.m.	
8:00	p.m.	
9:00	p.m.	
10:00	p.m.	
11:00	p.m.	
12:00	a.m.	

Daily Plan for Saturday, March 21, 2015

12:00	a.m.	
1:00	a.m.	
2:00	a.m.	
3:00	a.m.	
4:00	a.m.	
5:00	a.m.	
6:00	a.m.	
7:00	a.m.	
8:00	a.m.	
9:00	a.m.	
10:00	a.m.	
11:00	a.m.	
12:00	p.m.	
1:00	p.m.	
2:00	p.m.	
3:00	p.m.	
4:00	p.m.	
5:00	p.m.	
6:00	p.m.	
7:00	p.m.	
8:00	p.m.	
9:00	p.m.	
10:00	p.m.	
11:00	p.m.	
12:00	a.m.	

Daily Plan for Sunday, March 22, 2015

12:00	a.m.	
1:00	a.m.	
2:00	a.m.	
3:00	a.m.	
4:00	a.m.	
5:00	a.m.	
6:00	a.m.	
7:00	a.m.	
8:00	a.m.	
9:00	a.m.	
10:00	a.m.	
11:00	a.m.	
12:00	p.m.	
1:00	p.m.	
2:00	p.m.	
3:00	p.m.	
4:00	p.m.	
5:00	p.m.	
6:00	p.m.	
7:00	p.m.	
8:00	p.m.	
9:00	p.m.	
10:00	p.m.	
11:00	p.m.	
12:00	a.m.	

Daily Plan for Monday, March 23, 2015

12:00	a.m.	
1:00	a.m.	
2:00	a.m.	
3:00	a.m.	
4:00	a.m.	
5:00	a.m.	
6:00	a.m.	
7:00	a.m.	
8:00	a.m.	
9:00	a.m.	
10:00	a.m.	
11:00	a.m.	
12:00	p.m.	
1:00	p.m.	
2:00	p.m.	
3:00	p.m.	
4:00	p.m.	
5:00	p.m.	
6:00	p.m.	
7:00	p.m.	
8:00	p.m.	
9:00	p.m.	
10:00	p.m.	
11:00	p.m.	
12:00	a.m.	

Daily Plan for Tuesday, March 24, 2015

12:00	a.m.	
1:00	a.m.	
2:00	a.m.	
3:00	a.m.	
4:00	a.m.	
5:00	a.m.	
6:00	a.m.	
7:00	a.m.	
8:00	a.m.	
9:00	a.m.	
10:00	a.m.	
11:00	a.m.	
12:00	p.m.	
1:00	p.m.	
2:00	p.m.	
3:00	p.m.	
4:00	p.m.	
5:00	p.m.	
6:00	p.m.	
7:00	p.m.	
8:00	p.m.	
9:00	p.m.	
10:00	p.m.	
11:00	p.m.	
12:00	a.m.	

Daily Plan for Wednesday, March 25, 2015

12:00	a.m.	
1:00	a.m.	
2:00	a.m.	
3:00	a.m.	
4:00	a.m.	
5:00	a.m.	
6:00	a.m.	
7:00	a.m.	
8:00	a.m.	
9:00	a.m.	
10:00	a.m.	
11:00	a.m.	
12:00	p.m.	
1:00	p.m.	
2:00	p.m.	
3:00	p.m.	
4:00	p.m.	
5:00	p.m.	
6:00	p.m.	
7:00	p.m.	
8:00	p.m.	
9:00	p.m.	
10:00	p.m.	
11:00	p.m.	
12:00	a.m.	

Daily Plan for Thursday, March 26, 2015

12:00	a.m.	
1:00	a.m.	
2:00	a.m.	
3:00	a.m.	
4:00	a.m.	
5:00	a.m.	
6:00	a.m.	
7:00	a.m.	
8:00	a.m.	
9:00	a.m.	
10:00	a.m.	
11:00	a.m.	
12:00	p.m.	
1:00	p.m.	
2:00	p.m.	
3:00	p.m.	
4:00	p.m.	
5:00	p.m.	
6:00	p.m.	
7:00	p.m.	
8:00	p.m.	
9:00	p.m.	
10:00	p.m.	
11:00	p.m.	
12:00	a.m.	

Daily Plan for Friday, March 27, 2015

Time		
12:00	a.m.	
1:00	a.m.	
2:00	a.m.	
3:00	a.m.	
4:00	a.m.	
5:00	a.m.	
6:00	a.m.	
7:00	a.m.	
8:00	a.m.	
9:00	a.m.	
10:00	a.m.	
11:00	a.m.	
12:00	p.m.	
1:00	p.m.	
2:00	p.m.	
3:00	p.m.	
4:00	p.m.	
5:00	p.m.	
6:00	p.m.	
7:00	p.m.	
8:00	p.m.	
9:00	p.m.	
10:00	p.m.	
11:00	p.m.	
12:00	a.m.	

Daily Plan for Saturday, March 28, 2015

12:00	a.m.	
1:00	a.m.	
2:00	a.m.	
3:00	a.m.	
4:00	a.m.	
5:00	a.m.	
6:00	a.m.	
7:00	a.m.	
8:00	a.m.	
9:00	a.m.	
10:00	a.m.	
11:00	a.m.	
12:00	p.m.	
1:00	p.m.	
2:00	p.m.	
3:00	p.m.	
4:00	p.m.	
5:00	p.m.	
6:00	p.m.	
7:00	p.m.	
8:00	p.m.	
9:00	p.m.	
10:00	p.m.	
11:00	p.m.	
12:00	a.m.	

Daily Plan for Sunday, March 29, 2015

12:00	a.m.	
1:00	a.m.	
2:00	a.m.	
3:00	a.m.	
4:00	a.m.	
5:00	a.m.	
6:00	a.m.	
7:00	a.m.	
8:00	a.m.	
9:00	a.m.	
10:00	a.m.	
11:00	a.m.	
12:00	p.m.	
1:00	p.m.	
2:00	p.m.	
3:00	p.m.	
4:00	p.m.	
5:00	p.m.	
6:00	p.m.	
7:00	p.m.	
8:00	p.m.	
9:00	p.m.	
10:00	p.m.	
11:00	p.m.	
12:00	a.m.	

Daily Plan for Monday, March 30, 2015

12:00	a.m.	
1:00	a.m.	
2:00	a.m.	
3:00	a.m.	
4:00	a.m.	
5:00	a.m.	
6:00	a.m.	
7:00	a.m.	
8:00	a.m.	
9:00	a.m.	
10:00	a.m.	
11:00	a.m.	
12:00	p.m.	
1:00	p.m.	
2:00	p.m.	
3:00	p.m.	
4:00	p.m.	
5:00	p.m.	
6:00	p.m.	
7:00	p.m.	
8:00	p.m.	
9:00	p.m.	
10:00	p.m.	
11:00	p.m.	
12:00	a.m.	

Daily Plan for Tuesday, March 31, 2015

12:00	a.m.	
1:00	a.m.	
2:00	a.m.	
3:00	a.m.	
4:00	a.m.	
5:00	a.m.	
6:00	a.m.	
7:00	a.m.	
8:00	a.m.	
9:00	a.m.	
10:00	a.m.	
11:00	a.m.	
12:00	p.m.	
1:00	p.m.	
2:00	p.m.	
3:00	p.m.	
4:00	p.m.	
5:00	p.m.	
6:00	p.m.	
7:00	p.m.	
8:00	p.m.	
9:00	p.m.	
10:00	p.m.	
11:00	p.m.	
12:00	a.m.	

Daily Plan for Wednesday, April 1, 2015

12:00	a.m.	
1:00	a.m.	
2:00	a.m.	
3:00	a.m.	
4:00	a.m.	
5:00	a.m.	
6:00	a.m.	
7:00	a.m.	
8:00	a.m.	
9:00	a.m.	
10:00	a.m.	
11:00	a.m.	
12:00	p.m.	
1:00	p.m.	
2:00	p.m.	
3:00	p.m.	
4:00	p.m.	
5:00	p.m.	
6:00	p.m.	
7:00	p.m.	
8:00	p.m.	
9:00	p.m.	
10:00	p.m.	
11:00	p.m.	
12:00	a.m.	

Daily Plan for Thursday, April 2, 2015

12:00	a.m.	
1:00	a.m.	
2:00	a.m.	
3:00	a.m.	
4:00	a.m.	
5:00	a.m.	
6:00	a.m.	
7:00	a.m.	
8:00	a.m.	
9:00	a.m.	
10:00	a.m.	
11:00	a.m.	
12:00	p.m.	
1:00	p.m.	
2:00	p.m.	
3:00	p.m.	
4:00	p.m.	
5:00	p.m.	
6:00	p.m.	
7:00	p.m.	
8:00	p.m.	
9:00	p.m.	
10:00	p.m.	
11:00	p.m.	
12:00	a.m.	

Daily Plan for Friday, April 3, 2015

Time		
12:00	a.m.	
1:00	a.m.	
2:00	a.m.	
3:00	a.m.	
4:00	a.m.	
5:00	a.m.	
6:00	a.m.	
7:00	a.m.	
8:00	a.m.	
9:00	a.m.	
10:00	a.m.	
11:00	a.m.	
12:00	p.m.	
1:00	p.m.	
2:00	p.m.	
3:00	p.m.	
4:00	p.m.	
5:00	p.m.	
6:00	p.m.	
7:00	p.m.	
8:00	p.m.	
9:00	p.m.	
10:00	p.m.	
11:00	p.m.	
12:00	a.m.	

Daily Plan for Saturday, April 4, 2015

12:00	a.m.	
1:00	a.m.	
2:00	a.m.	
3:00	a.m.	
4:00	a.m.	
5:00	a.m.	
6:00	a.m.	
7:00	a.m.	
8:00	a.m.	
9:00	a.m.	
10:00	a.m.	
11:00	a.m.	
12:00	p.m.	
1:00	p.m.	
2:00	p.m.	
3:00	p.m.	
4:00	p.m.	
5:00	p.m.	
6:00	p.m.	
7:00	p.m.	
8:00	p.m.	
9:00	p.m.	
10:00	p.m.	
11:00	p.m.	
12:00	a.m.	

Daily Plan for Sunday, April 5, 2015

12:00	a.m.	
1:00	a.m.	
2:00	a.m.	
3:00	a.m.	
4:00	a.m.	
5:00	a.m.	
6:00	a.m.	
7:00	a.m.	
8:00	a.m.	
9:00	a.m.	
10:00	a.m.	
11:00	a.m.	
12:00	p.m.	
1:00	p.m.	
2:00	p.m.	
3:00	p.m.	
4:00	p.m.	
5:00	p.m.	
6:00	p.m.	
7:00	p.m.	
8:00	p.m.	
9:00	p.m.	
10:00	p.m.	
11:00	p.m.	
12:00	a.m.	

Daily Plan for Monday, April 6, 2015

12:00	a.m.	
1:00	a.m.	
2:00	a.m.	
3:00	a.m.	
4:00	a.m.	
5:00	a.m.	
6:00	a.m.	
7:00	a.m.	
8:00	a.m.	
9:00	a.m.	
10:00	a.m.	
11:00	a.m.	
12:00	p.m.	
1:00	p.m.	
2:00	p.m.	
3:00	p.m.	
4:00	p.m.	
5:00	p.m.	
6:00	p.m.	
7:00	p.m.	
8:00	p.m.	
9:00	p.m.	
10:00	p.m.	
11:00	p.m.	
12:00	a.m.	

Daily Plan for Tuesday, April 7, 2015

12:00	a.m.	
1:00	a.m.	
2:00	a.m.	
3:00	a.m.	
4:00	a.m.	
5:00	a.m.	
6:00	a.m.	
7:00	a.m.	
8:00	a.m.	
9:00	a.m.	
10:00	a.m.	
11:00	a.m.	
12:00	p.m.	
1:00	p.m.	
2:00	p.m.	
3:00	p.m.	
4:00	p.m.	
5:00	p.m.	
6:00	p.m.	
7:00	p.m.	
8:00	p.m.	
9:00	p.m.	
10:00	p.m.	
11:00	p.m.	
12:00	a.m.	

Daily Plan for Wednesday, April 8, 2015

12:00	a.m.	
1:00	a.m.	
2:00	a.m.	
3:00	a.m.	
4:00	a.m.	
5:00	a.m.	
6:00	a.m.	
7:00	a.m.	
8:00	a.m.	
9:00	a.m.	
10:00	a.m.	
11:00	a.m.	
12:00	p.m.	
1:00	p.m.	
2:00	p.m.	
3:00	p.m.	
4:00	p.m.	
5:00	p.m.	
6:00	p.m.	
7:00	p.m.	
8:00	p.m.	
9:00	p.m.	
10:00	p.m.	
11:00	p.m.	
12:00	a.m.	

Daily Plan for Thursday, April 9, 2015

Time		
12:00	a.m.	
1:00	a.m.	
2:00	a.m.	
3:00	a.m.	
4:00	a.m.	
5:00	a.m.	
6:00	a.m.	
7:00	a.m.	
8:00	a.m.	
9:00	a.m.	
10:00	a.m.	
11:00	a.m.	
12:00	p.m.	
1:00	p.m.	
2:00	p.m.	
3:00	p.m.	
4:00	p.m.	
5:00	p.m.	
6:00	p.m.	
7:00	p.m.	
8:00	p.m.	
9:00	p.m.	
10:00	p.m.	
11:00	p.m.	
12:00	a.m.	

Daily Plan for Friday, April 10, 2015

12:00	a.m.	
1:00	a.m.	
2:00	a.m.	
3:00	a.m.	
4:00	a.m.	
5:00	a.m.	
6:00	a.m.	
7:00	a.m.	
8:00	a.m.	
9:00	a.m.	
10:00	a.m.	
11:00	a.m.	
12:00	p.m.	
1:00	p.m.	
2:00	p.m.	
3:00	p.m.	
4:00	p.m.	
5:00	p.m.	
6:00	p.m.	
7:00	p.m.	
8:00	p.m.	
9:00	p.m.	
10:00	p.m.	
11:00	p.m.	
12:00	a.m.	

Daily Plan for Saturday, April 11, 2015

12:00	a.m.	
1:00	a.m.	
2:00	a.m.	
3:00	a.m.	
4:00	a.m.	
5:00	a.m.	
6:00	a.m.	
7:00	a.m.	
8:00	a.m.	
9:00	a.m.	
10:00	a.m.	
11:00	a.m.	
12:00	p.m.	
1:00	p.m.	
2:00	p.m.	
3:00	p.m.	
4:00	p.m.	
5:00	p.m.	
6:00	p.m.	
7:00	p.m.	
8:00	p.m.	
9:00	p.m.	
10:00	p.m.	
11:00	p.m.	
12:00	a.m.	

Daily Plan for Sunday, April 12, 2015

12:00	a.m.	
1:00	a.m.	
2:00	a.m.	
3:00	a.m.	
p4:00	a.m.	
5:00	a.m.	
6:00	a.m.	
7:00	a.m.	
8:00	a.m.	
9:00	a.m.	
10:00	a.m.	
11:00	a.m.	
12:00	p.m.	
1:00	p.m.	
2:00	p.m.	
3:00	p.m.	
4:00	p.m.	
5:00	p.m.	
6:00	p.m.	
7:00	p.m.	
8:00	p.m.	
9:00	p.m.	
10:00	p.m.	
11:00	p.m.	
12:00	a.m.	

Daily Plan for Monday, April 13, 2015

12:00	a.m.	
1:00	a.m.	
2:00	a.m.	
3:00	a.m.	
4:00	a.m.	
5:00	a.m.	
6:00	a.m.	
7:00	a.m.	
8:00	a.m.	
9:00	a.m.	
10:00	a.m.	
11:00	a.m.	
12:00	p.m.	
1:00	p.m.	
2:00	p.m.	
3:00	p.m.	
4:00	p.m.	
5:00	p.m.	
6:00	p.m.	
7:00	p.m.	
8:00	p.m.	
9:00	p.m.	
10:00	p.m.	
11:00	p.m.	
12:00	a.m.	

Daily Plan for Tuesday, April 14, 2015

12:00	a.m.	
1:00	a.m.	
2:00	a.m.	
3:00	a.m.	
4:00	a.m.	
5:00	a.m.	
6:00	a.m.	
7:00	a.m.	
8:00	a.m.	
9:00	a.m.	
10:00	a.m.	
11:00	a.m.	
12:00	p.m.	
1:00	p.m.	
2:00	p.m.	
3:00	p.m.	
4:00	p.m.	
5:00	p.m.	
6:00	p.m.	
7:00	p.m.	
8:00	p.m.	
9:00	p.m.	
10:00	p.m.	
11:00	p.m.	
12:00	a.m.	

Daily Plan for Wednesday, April 15, 2015

12:00	a.m.	
1:00	a.m.	
2:00	a.m.	
3:00	a.m.	
4:00	a.m.	
5:00	a.m.	
6:00	a.m.	
7:00	a.m.	
8:00	a.m.	
9:00	a.m.	
10:00	a.m.	
11:00	a.m.	
12:00	p.m.	
1:00	p.m.	
2:00	p.m.	
3:00	p.m.	
4:00	p.m.	
5:00	p.m.	
6:00	p.m.	
7:00	p.m.	
8:00	p.m.	
9:00	p.m.	
10:00	p.m.	
11:00	p.m.	
12:00	a.m.	

Daily Plan for Thursday, April 16, 2015

12:00	a.m.	
1:00	a.m.	
2:00	a.m.	
3:00	a.m.	
4:00	a.m.	
5:00	a.m.	
6:00	a.m.	
7:00	a.m.	
8:00	a.m.	
9:00	a.m.	
10:00	a.m.	
11:00	a.m.	
12:00	p.m.	
1:00	p.m.	
2:00	p.m.	
3:00	p.m.	
4:00	p.m.	
5:00	p.m.	
6:00	p.m.	
7:00	p.m.	
8:00	p.m.	
9:00	p.m.	
10:00	p.m.	
11:00	p.m.	
12:00	a.m.	

Daily Plan for Friday, April 17, 2015

12:00	a.m.	
1:00	a.m.	
2:00	a.m.	
3:00	a.m.	
4:00	a.m.	
5:00	a.m.	
6:00	a.m.	
7:00	a.m.	
8:00	a.m.	
9:00	a.m.	
10:00	a.m.	
11:00	a.m.	
12:00	p.m.	
1:00	p.m.	
2:00	p.m.	
3:00	p.m.	
4:00	p.m.	
5:00	p.m.	
6:00	p.m.	
7:00	p.m.	
8:00	p.m.	
9:00	p.m.	
10:00	p.m.	
11:00	p.m.	
12:00	a.m.	

Daily Plan for Saturday, April 18, 2015

12:00	a.m.	
1:00	a.m.	
2:00	a.m.	
3:00	a.m.	
4:00	a.m.	
5:00	a.m.	
6:00	a.m.	
7:00	a.m.	
8:00	a.m.	
9:00	a.m.	
10:00	a.m.	
11:00	a.m.	
12:00	p.m.	
1:00	p.m.	
2:00	p.m.	
3:00	p.m.	
4:00	p.m.	
5:00	p.m.	
6:00	p.m.	
7:00	p.m.	
8:00	p.m.	
9:00	p.m.	
10:00	p.m.	
11:00	p.m.	
12:00	a.m.	

Daily Plan for Sunday, April 19, 2015

12:00	a.m.	
1:00	a.m.	
2:00	a.m.	
3:00	a.m.	
4:00	a.m.	
5:00	a.m.	
6:00	a.m.	
7:00	a.m.	
8:00	a.m.	
9:00	a.m.	
10:00	a.m.	
11:00	a.m.	
12:00	p.m.	
1:00	p.m.	
2:00	p.m.	
3:00	p.m.	
4:00	p.m.	
5:00	p.m.	
6:00	p.m.	
7:00	p.m.	
8:00	p.m.	
9:00	p.m.	
10:00	p.m.	
11:00	p.m.	
12:00	a.m.	

Daily Plan for Monday, April 20, 2015

12:00	a.m.	
1:00	a.m.	
2:00	a.m.	
3:00	a.m.	
4:00	a.m.	
5:00	a.m.	
6:00	a.m.	
7:00	a.m.	
8:00	a.m.	
9:00	a.m.	
10:00	a.m.	
11:00	a.m.	
12:00	p.m.	
1:00	p.m.	
2:00	p.m.	
3:00	p.m.	
4:00	p.m.	
5:00	p.m.	
6:00	p.m.	
7:00	p.m.	
8:00	p.m.	
9:00	p.m.	
10:00	p.m.	
11:00	p.m.	
12:00	a.m.	

Daily Plan for Tuesday, April 21, 2015

12:00	a.m.	
1:00	a.m.	
2:00	a.m.	
3:00	a.m.	
4:00	a.m.	
5:00	a.m.	
6:00	a.m.	
7:00	a.m.	
8:00	a.m.	
9:00	a.m.	
10:00	a.m.	
11:00	a.m.	
12:00	p.m.	
1:00	p.m.	
2:00	p.m.	
3:00	p.m.	
4:00	p.m.	
5:00	p.m.	
6:00	p.m.	
7:00	p.m.	
8:00	p.m.	
9:00	p.m.	
10:00	p.m.	
11:00	p.m.	
12:00	a.m.	

Daily Plan for Wednesday, April 22, 2015

12:00	a.m.	
1:00	a.m.	
2:00	a.m.	
3:00	a.m.	
4:00	a.m.	
5:00	a.m.	
6:00	a.m.	
7:00	a.m.	
8:00	a.m.	
9:00	a.m.	
10:00	a.m.	
11:00	a.m.	
12:00	p.m.	
1:00	p.m.	
2:00	p.m.	
3:00	p.m.	
4:00	p.m.	
5:00	p.m.	
6:00	p.m.	
7:00	p.m.	
8:00	p.m.	
9:00	p.m.	
10:00	p.m.	
11:00	p.m.	
12:00	a.m.	

Daily Plan for Thursday, April 23, 2015

12:00	a.m.	
1:00	a.m.	
2:00	a.m.	
3:00	a.m.	
4:00	a.m.	
5:00	a.m.	
6:00	a.m.	
7:00	a.m.	
8:00	a.m.	
9:00	a.m.	
10:00	a.m.	
11:00	a.m.	
12:00	p.m.	
1:00	p.m.	
2:00	p.m.	
3:00	p.m.	
4:00	p.m.	
5:00	p.m.	
6:00	p.m.	
7:00	p.m.	
8:00	p.m.	
9:00	p.m.	
10:00	p.m.	
11:00	p.m.	
12:00	a.m.	

Daily Plan for Friday, April 24, 2015

12:00	a.m.	
1:00	a.m.	
2:00	a.m.	
3:00	a.m.	
4:00	a.m.	
5:00	a.m.	
6:00	a.m.	
7:00	a.m.	
8:00	a.m.	
9:00	a.m.	
10:00	a.m.	
11:00	a.m.	
12:00	p.m.	
1:00	p.m.	
2:00	p.m.	
3:00	p.m.	
4:00	p.m.	
5:00	p.m.	
6:00	p.m.	
7:00	p.m.	
8:00	p.m.	
9:00	p.m.	
10:00	p.m.	
11:00	p.m.	
12:00	a.m.	

Daily Plan for Saturday, April 25, 2015

12:00	a.m.	
1:00	a.m.	
2:00	a.m.	
3:00	a.m.	
4:00	a.m.	
5:00	a.m.	
6:00	a.m.	
7:00	a.m.	
8:00	a.m.	
9:00	a.m.	
10:00	a.m.	
11:00	a.m.	
12:00	p.m.	
1:00	p.m.	
2:00	p.m.	
3:00	p.m.	
4:00	p.m.	
5:00	p.m.	
6:00	p.m.	
7:00	p.m.	
8:00	p.m.	
9:00	p.m.	
10:00	p.m.	
11:00	p.m.	
12:00	a.m.	

Daily Plan for Sunday, April 26, 2015

Time		
12:00	a.m.	
1:00	a.m.	
2:00	a.m.	
3:00	a.m.	
4:00	a.m.	
5:00	a.m.	
6:00	a.m.	
7:00	a.m.	
8:00	a.m.	
9:00	a.m.	
10:00	a.m.	
11:00	a.m.	
12:00	p.m.	
1:00	p.m.	
2:00	p.m.	
3:00	p.m.	
4:00	p.m.	
5:00	p.m.	
6:00	p.m.	
7:00	p.m.	
8:00	p.m.	
9:00	p.m.	
10:00	p.m.	
11:00	p.m.	
12:00	a.m.	

Daily Plan for Monday, April 27, 2015

12:00	a.m.	
1:00	a.m.	
2:00	a.m.	
3:00	a.m.	
4:00	a.m.	
5:00	a.m.	
6:00	a.m.	
7:00	a.m.	
8:00	a.m.	
9:00	a.m.	
10:00	a.m.	
11:00	a.m.	
12:00	p.m.	
1:00	p.m.	
2:00	p.m.	
3:00	p.m.	
4:00	p.m.	
5:00	p.m.	
6:00	p.m.	
7:00	p.m.	
8:00	p.m.	
9:00	p.m.	
10:00	p.m.	
11:00	p.m.	
12:00	a.m.	

Daily Plan for Tuesday, April 28, 2015

12:00	a.m.	
1:00	a.m.	
2:00	a.m.	
3:00	a.m.	
4:00	a.m.	
5:00	a.m.	
6:00	a.m.	
7:00	a.m.	
8:00	a.m.	
9:00	a.m.	
10:00	a.m.	
11:00	a.m.	
12:00	p.m.	
1:00	p.m.	
2:00	p.m.	
3:00	p.m.	
4:00	p.m.	
5:00	p.m.	
6:00	p.m.	
7:00	p.m.	
8:00	p.m.	
9:00	p.m.	
10:00	p.m.	
11:00	p.m.	
12:00	a.m.	

Daily Plan for Wednesday, April 29, 2015

12:00 a.m.	
1:00 a.m.	
2:00 a.m.	
3:00 a.m.	
4:00 a.m.	
5:00 a.m.	
6:00 a.m.	
7:00 a.m.	
8:00 a.m.	
9:00 a.m.	
10:00 a.m.	
11:00 a.m.	
12:00 p.m.	
1:00 p.m.	
2:00 p.m.	
3:00 p.m.	
4:00 p.m.	
5:00 p.m.	
6:00 p.m.	
7:00 p.m.	
8:00 p.m.	
9:00 p.m.	
10:00 p.m.	
11:00 p.m.	
12:00 a.m.	

Daily Plan for Thursday, April 30, 2015

Time		
12:00	a.m.	
1:00	a.m.	
2:00	a.m.	
3:00	a.m.	
4:00	a.m.	
5:00	a.m.	
6:00	a.m.	
7:00	a.m.	
8:00	a.m.	
9:00	a.m.	
10:00	a.m.	
11:00	a.m.	
12:00	p.m.	
1:00	p.m.	
2:00	p.m.	
3:00	p.m.	
4:00	p.m.	
5:00	p.m.	
6:00	p.m.	
7:00	p.m.	
8:00	p.m.	
9:00	p.m.	
10:00	p.m.	
11:00	p.m.	
12:00	a.m.	

Daily Plan for Friday, May 1, 2015

12:00	a.m.	
1:00	a.m.	
2:00	a.m.	
3:00	a.m.	
4:00	a.m.	
5:00	a.m.	
6:00	a.m.	
7:00	a.m.	
8:00	a.m.	
9:00	a.m.	
10:00	a.m.	
11:00	a.m.	
12:00	p.m.	
1:00	p.m.	
2:00	p.m.	
3:00	p.m.	
4:00	p.m.	
5:00	p.m.	
6:00	p.m.	
7:00	p.m.	
8:00	p.m.	
9:00	p.m.	
10:00	p.m.	
11:00	p.m.	
12:00	a.m.	

Daily Plan for Saturday, May 2, 2015

12:00	a.m.	
1:00	a.m.	
2:00	a.m.	
3:00	a.m.	
4:00	a.m.	
5:00	a.m.	
6:00	a.m.	
7:00	a.m.	
8:00	a.m.	
9:00	a.m.	
10:00	a.m.	
11:00	a.m.	
12:00	p.m.	
1:00	p.m.	
2:00	p.m.	
3:00	p.m.	
4:00	p.m.	
5:00	p.m.	
6:00	p.m.	
7:00	p.m.	
8:00	p.m.	
9:00	p.m.	
10:00	p.m.	
11:00	p.m.	
12:00	a.m.	

Daily Plan for Sunday, May 3, 2015

12:00	a.m.	
1:00	a.m.	
2:00	a.m.	
3:00	a.m.	
4:00	a.m.	
5:00	a.m.	
6:00	a.m.	
7:00	a.m.	
8:00	a.m.	
9:00	a.m.	
10:00	a.m.	
11:00	a.m.	
12:00	p.m.	
1:00	p.m.	
2:00	p.m.	
3:00	p.m.	
4:00	p.m.	
5:00	p.m.	
6:00	p.m.	
7:00	p.m.	
8:00	p.m.	
9:00	p.m.	
10:00	p.m.	
11:00	p.m.	
12:00	a.m.	

Daily Plan for Monday, May 4, 2015

12:00	a.m.	
1:00	a.m.	
2:00	a.m.	
3:00	a.m.	
4:00	a.m.	
5:00	a.m.	
6:00	a.m.	
7:00	a.m.	
8:00	a.m.	
9:00	a.m.	
10:00	a.m.	
11:00	a.m.	
12:00	p.m.	
1:00	p.m.	
2:00	p.m.	
3:00	p.m.	
4:00	p.m.	
5:00	p.m.	
6:00	p.m.	
7:00	p.m.	
8:00	p.m.	
9:00	p.m.	
10:00	p.m.	
11:00	p.m.	
12:00	a.m.	

Daily Plan for Tuesday, May 5, 2015

Time	
12:00 a.m.	
1:00 a.m.	
2:00 a.m.	
3:00 a.m.	
4:00 a.m.	
5:00 a.m.	
6:00 a.m.	
7:00 a.m.	
8:00 a.m.	
9:00 a.m.	
10:00 a.m.	
11:00 a.m.	
12:00 p.m.	
1:00 p.m.	
2:00 p.m.	
3:00 p.m.	
4:00 p.m.	
5:00 p.m.	
6:00 p.m.	
7:00 p.m.	
8:00 p.m.	
9:00 p.m.	
10:00 p.m.	
11:00 p.m.	
12:00 a.m.	

Daily Plan for Wednesday, May 6, 2015

Time		
12:00	a.m.	
1:00	a.m.	
2:00	a.m.	
3:00	a.m.	
4:00	a.m.	
5:00	a.m.	
6:00	a.m.	
7:00	a.m.	
8:00	a.m.	
9:00	a.m.	
10:00	a.m.	
11:00	a.m.	
12:00	p.m.	
1:00	p.m.	
2:00	p.m.	
3:00	p.m.	
4:00	p.m.	
5:00	p.m.	
6:00	p.m.	
7:00	p.m.	
8:00	p.m.	
9:00	p.m.	
10:00	p.m.	
11:00	p.m.	
12:00	a.m.	

Daily Plan for Thursday, May 7, 2015

12:00	a.m.	
1:00	a.m.	
2:00	a.m.	
3:00	a.m.	
4:00	a.m.	
5:00	a.m.	
6:00	a.m.	
7:00	a.m.	
8:00	a.m.	
9:00	a.m.	
10:00	a.m.	
11:00	a.m.	
12:00	p.m.	
1:00	p.m.	
2:00	p.m.	
3:00	p.m.	
4:00	p.m.	
5:00	p.m.	
6:00	p.m.	
7:00	p.m.	
8:00	p.m.	
9:00	p.m.	
10:00	p.m.	
11:00	p.m.	
12:00	a.m.	

Daily Plan for Friday, May 8, 2015

12:00	a.m.	
1:00	a.m.	
2:00	a.m.	
3:00	a.m.	
4:00	a.m.	
5:00	a.m.	
6:00	a.m.	
7:00	a.m.	
8:00	a.m.	
9:00	a.m.	
10:00	a.m.	
11:00	a.m.	
12:00	p.m.	
1:00	p.m.	
2:00	p.m.	
3:00	p.m.	
4:00	p.m.	
5:00	p.m.	
6:00	p.m.	
7:00	p.m.	
8:00	p.m.	
9:00	p.m.	
10:00	p.m.	
11:00	p.m.	
12:00	a.m.	

Daily Plan for Saturday, May 9, 2015

12:00	a.m.	
1:00	a.m.	
2:00	a.m.	
3:00	a.m.	
4:00	a.m.	
5:00	a.m.	
6:00	a.m.	
7:00	a.m.	
8:00	a.m.	
9:00	a.m.	
10:00	a.m.	
11:00	a.m.	
12:00	p.m.	
1:00	p.m.	
2:00	p.m.	
3:00	p.m.	
4:00	p.m.	
5:00	p.m.	
6:00	p.m.	
7:00	p.m.	
8:00	p.m.	
9:00	p.m.	
10:00	p.m.	
11:00	p.m.	
12:00	a.m.	

Daily Plan for Sunday, May 10, 2015

12:00	a.m.	
1:00	a.m.	
2:00	a.m.	
3:00	a.m.	
4:00	a.m.	
5:00	a.m.	
6:00	a.m.	
7:00	a.m.	
8:00	a.m.	
9:00	a.m.	
10:00	a.m.	
11:00	a.m.	
12:00	p.m.	
1:00	p.m.	
2:00	p.m.	
3:00	p.m.	
4:00	p.m.	
5:00	p.m.	
6:00	p.m.	
7:00	p.m.	
8:00	p.m.	
9:00	p.m.	
10:00	p.m.	
11:00	p.m.	
12:00	a.m.	

Daily Plan for Monday, May 11, 2015

12:00	a.m.	
1:00	a.m.	
2:00	a.m.	
3:00	a.m.	
4:00	a.m.	
5:00	a.m.	
6:00	a.m.	
7:00	a.m.	
8:00	a.m.	
9:00	a.m.	
10:00	a.m.	
11:00	a.m.	
12:00	p.m.	
1:00	p.m.	
2:00	p.m.	
3:00	p.m.	
4:00	p.m.	
5:00	p.m.	
6:00	p.m.	
7:00	p.m.	
8:00	p.m.	
9:00	p.m.	
10:00	p.m.	
11:00	p.m.	
12:00	a.m.	

Daily Plan for Tuesday, May 12, 2015

12:00	a.m.	
1:00	a.m.	
2:00	a.m.	
3:00	a.m.	
4:00	a.m.	
5:00	a.m.	
6:00	a.m.	
7:00	a.m.	
8:00	a.m.	
9:00	a.m.	
10:00	a.m.	
11:00	a.m.	
12:00	p.m.	
1:00	p.m.	
2:00	p.m.	
3:00	p.m.	
4:00	p.m.	
5:00	p.m.	
6:00	p.m.	
7:00	p.m.	
8:00	p.m.	
9:00	p.m.	
10:00	p.m.	
11:00	p.m.	
12:00	a.m.	

Daily Plan for Wednesday, May 13, 2015

12:00	a.m.	
1:00	a.m.	
2:00	a.m.	
3:00	a.m.	
4:00	a.m.	
5:00	a.m.	
6:00	a.m.	
7:00	a.m.	
8:00	a.m.	
9:00	a.m.	
10:00	a.m.	
11:00	a.m.	
12:00	p.m.	
1:00	p.m.	
2:00	p.m.	
3:00	p.m.	
4:00	p.m.	
5:00	p.m.	
6:00	p.m.	
7:00	p.m.	
8:00	p.m.	
9:00	p.m.	
10:00	p.m.	
11:00	p.m.	
12:00	a.m.	

Daily Plan for Thursday, May 14, 2015

12:00	a.m.	
1:00	a.m.	
2:00	a.m.	
3:00	a.m.	
4:00	a.m.	
5:00	a.m.	
6:00	a.m.	
7:00	a.m.	
8:00	a.m.	
9:00	a.m.	
10:00	a.m.	
11:00	a.m.	
12:00	p.m.	
1:00	p.m.	
2:00	p.m.	
3:00	p.m.	
4:00	p.m.	
5:00	p.m.	
6:00	p.m.	
7:00	p.m.	
8:00	p.m.	
9:00	p.m.	
10:00	p.m.	
11:00	p.m.	
12:00	a.m.	

Daily Plan for Friday, May 15, 2015

12:00	a.m.	
1:00	a.m.	
2:00	a.m.	
3:00	a.m.	
4:00	a.m.	
5:00	a.m.	
6:00	a.m.	
7:00	a.m.	
8:00	a.m.	
9:00	a.m.	
10:00	a.m.	
11:00	a.m.	
12:00	p.m.	
1:00	p.m.	
2:00	p.m.	
3:00	p.m.	
4:00	p.m.	
5:00	p.m.	
6:00	p.m.	
7:00	p.m.	
8:00	p.m.	
9:00	p.m.	
10:00	p.m.	
11:00	p.m.	
12:00	a.m.	

Daily Plan for Saturday, May 16, 2015

12:00	a.m.	
1:00	a.m.	
2:00	a.m.	
3:00	a.m.	
4:00	a.m.	
5:00	a.m.	
6:00	a.m.	
7:00	a.m.	
8:00	a.m.	
9:00	a.m.	
10:00	a.m.	
11:00	a.m.	
12:00	p.m.	
1:00	p.m.	
2:00	p.m.	
3:00	p.m.	
4:00	p.m.	
5:00	p.m.	
6:00	p.m.	
7:00	p.m.	
8:00	p.m.	
9:00	p.m.	
10:00	p.m.	
11:00	p.m.	
12:00	a.m.	

Daily Plan for Sunday, May 17, 2015

12:00	a.m.	
1:00	a.m.	
2:00	a.m.	
3:00	a.m.	
4:00	a.m.	
5:00	a.m.	
6:00	a.m.	
7:00	a.m.	
8:00	a.m.	
9:00	a.m.	
10:00	a.m.	
11:00	a.m.	
12:00	p.m.	
1:00	p.m.	
2:00	p.m.	
3:00	p.m.	
4:00	p.m.	
5:00	p.m.	
6:00	p.m.	
7:00	p.m.	
8:00	p.m.	
9:00	p.m.	
10:00	p.m.	
11:00	p.m.	
12:00	a.m.	

Daily Plan for Monday, May 18, 2015

12:00	a.m.	
1:00	a.m.	
2:00	a.m.	
3:00	a.m.	
4:00	a.m.	
5:00	a.m.	
6:00	a.m.	
7:00	a.m.	
8:00	a.m.	
9:00	a.m.	
10:00	a.m.	
11:00	a.m.	
12:00	p.m.	
1:00	p.m.	
2:00	p.m.	
3:00	p.m.	
4:00	p.m.	
5:00	p.m.	
6:00	p.m.	
7:00	p.m.	
8:00	p.m.	
9:00	p.m.	
10:00	p.m.	
11:00	p.m.	
12:00	a.m.	

Daily Plan for Tuesday, May 19, 2015

12:00	a.m.	
1:00	a.m.	
2:00	a.m.	
3:00	a.m.	
4:00	a.m.	
5:00	a.m.	
6:00	a.m.	
7:00	a.m.	
8:00	a.m.	
9:00	a.m.	
10:00	a.m.	
11:00	a.m.	
12:00	p.m.	
1:00	p.m.	
2:00	p.m.	
3:00	p.m.	
4:00	p.m.	
5:00	p.m.	
6:00	p.m.	
7:00	p.m.	
8:00	p.m.	
9:00	p.m.	
10:00	p.m.	
11:00	p.m.	
12:00	a.m.	

Daily Plan for Wednesday, May 20, 2015

12:00	a.m.	
1:00	a.m.	
2:00	a.m.	
3:00	a.m.	
4:00	a.m.	
5:00	a.m.	
6:00	a.m.	
7:00	a.m.	
8:00	a.m.	
9:00	a.m.	
10:00	a.m.	
11:00	a.m.	
12:00	p.m.	
1:00	p.m.	
2:00	p.m.	
3:00	p.m.	
4:00	p.m.	
5:00	p.m.	
6:00	p.m.	
7:00	p.m.	
8:00	p.m.	
9:00	p.m.	
10:00	p.m.	
11:00	p.m.	
12:00	a.m.	

Daily Plan for Thursday, May 21, 2015

12:00	a.m.	
1:00	a.m.	
2:00	a.m.	
3:00	a.m.	
4:00	a.m.	
5:00	a.m.	
6:00	a.m.	
7:00	a.m.	
8:00	a.m.	
9:00	a.m.	
10:00	a.m.	
11:00	a.m.	
12:00	p.m.	
1:00	p.m.	
2:00	p.m.	
3:00	p.m.	
4:00	p.m.	
5:00	p.m.	
6:00	p.m.	
7:00	p.m.	
8:00	p.m.	
9:00	p.m.	
10:00	p.m.	
11:00	p.m.	
12:00	a.m.	

Daily Plan for Friday, May 22, 2015

12:00	a.m.	
1:00	a.m.	
2:00	a.m.	
3:00	a.m.	
4:00	a.m.	
5:00	a.m.	
6:00	a.m.	
7:00	a.m.	
8:00	a.m.	
9:00	a.m.	
10:00	a.m.	
11:00	a.m.	
12:00	p.m.	
1:00	p.m.	
2:00	p.m.	
3:00	p.m.	
4:00	p.m.	
5:00	p.m.	
6:00	p.m.	
7:00	p.m.	
8:00	p.m.	
9:00	p.m.	
10:00	p.m.	
11:00	p.m.	
12:00	a.m.	

Daily Plan for Saturday, May 23, 2015

12:00	a.m.	
1:00	a.m.	
2:00	a.m.	
3:00	a.m.	
4:00	a.m.	
5:00	a.m.	
6:00	a.m.	
7:00	a.m.	
8:00	a.m.	
9:00	a.m.	
10:00	a.m.	
11:00	a.m.	
12:00	p.m.	
1:00	p.m.	
2:00	p.m.	
3:00	p.m.	
4:00	p.m.	
5:00	p.m.	
6:00	p.m.	
7:00	p.m.	
8:00	p.m.	
9:00	p.m.	
10:00	p.m.	
11:00	p.m.	
12:00	a.m.	

Daily Plan for Sunday, May 24, 2015

12:00	a.m.	
1:00	a.m.	
2:00	a.m.	
3:00	a.m.	
4:00	a.m.	
5:00	a.m.	
6:00	a.m.	
7:00	a.m.	
8:00	a.m.	
9:00	a.m.	
10:00	a.m.	
11:00	a.m.	
12:00	p.m.	
1:00	p.m.	
2:00	p.m.	
3:00	p.m.	
4:00	p.m.	
5:00	p.m.	
6:00	p.m.	
7:00	p.m.	
8:00	p.m.	
9:00	p.m.	
10:00	p.m.	
11:00	p.m.	
12:00	a.m.	

Daily Plan for Monday, May 25, 2015

12:00	a.m.	
1:00	a.m.	
2:00	a.m.	
3:00	a.m.	
4:00	a.m.	
5:00	a.m.	
6:00	a.m.	
7:00	a.m.	
8:00	a.m.	
9:00	a.m.	
10:00	a.m.	
11:00	a.m.	
12:00	p.m.	
1:00	p.m.	
2:00	p.m.	
3:00	p.m.	
4:00	p.m.	
5:00	p.m.	
6:00	p.m.	
7:00	p.m.	
8:00	p.m.	
9:00	p.m.	
10:00	p.m.	
11:00	p.m.	
12:00	a.m.	

Daily Plan for Tuesday, May 26, 2015

12:00	a.m.	
1:00	a.m.	
2:00	a.m.	
3:00	a.m.	
4:00	a.m.	
5:00	a.m.	
6:00	a.m.	
7:00	a.m.	
8:00	a.m.	
9:00	a.m.	
10:00	a.m.	
11:00	a.m.	
12:00	p.m.	
1:00	p.m.	
2:00	p.m.	
3:00	p.m.	
4:00	p.m.	
5:00	p.m.	
6:00	p.m.	
7:00	p.m.	
8:00	p.m.	
9:00	p.m.	
10:00	p.m.	
11:00	p.m.	
12:00	a.m.	

Daily Plan for Wednesday, May 27, 2015

12:00 a.m.	
1:00 a.m.	
2:00 a.m.	
3:00 a.m.	
4:00 a.m.	
5:00 a.m.	
6:00 a.m.	
7:00 a.m.	
8:00 a.m.	
9:00 a.m.	
10:00 a.m.	
11:00 a.m.	
12:00 p.m.	
1:00 p.m.	
2:00 p.m.	
3:00 p.m.	
4:00 p.m.	
5:00 p.m.	
6:00 p.m.	
7:00 p.m.	
8:00 p.m.	
9:00 p.m.	
10:00 p.m.	
11:00 p.m.	
12:00 a.m.	

Daily Plan for Thursday, May 28, 2015

12:00	a.m.	
1:00	a.m.	
2:00	a.m.	
3:00	a.m.	
4:00	a.m.	
5:00	a.m.	
6:00	a.m.	
7:00	a.m.	
8:00	a.m.	
9:00	a.m.	
10:00	a.m.	
11:00	a.m.	
12:00	p.m.	
1:00	p.m.	
2:00	p.m.	
3:00	p.m.	
4:00	p.m.	
5:00	p.m.	
6:00	p.m.	
7:00	p.m.	
8:00	p.m.	
9:00	p.m.	
10:00	p.m.	
11:00	p.m.	
12:00	a.m.	

Daily Plan for Friday, May 29, 2015

12:00	a.m.	
1:00	a.m.	
2:00	a.m.	
3:00	a.m.	
4:00	a.m.	
5:00	a.m.	
6:00	a.m.	
7:00	a.m.	
8:00	a.m.	
9:00	a.m.	
10:00	a.m.	
11:00	a.m.	
12:00	p.m.	
1:00	p.m.	
2:00	p.m.	
3:00	p.m.	
4:00	p.m.	
5:00	p.m.	
6:00	p.m.	
7:00	p.m.	
8:00	p.m.	
9:00	p.m.	
10:00	p.m.	
11:00	p.m.	
12:00	a.m.	

Daily Plan for Saturday, May 30, 2015

12:00	a.m.	
1:00	a.m.	
2:00	a.m.	
3:00	a.m.	
4:00	a.m.	
5:00	a.m.	
6:00	a.m.	
7:00	a.m.	
8:00	a.m.	
9:00	a.m.	
10:00	a.m.	
11:00	a.m.	
12:00	p.m.	
1:00	p.m.	
2:00	p.m.	
3:00	p.m.	
4:00	p.m.	
5:00	p.m.	
6:00	p.m.	
7:00	p.m.	
8:00	p.m.	
9:00	p.m.	
10:00	p.m.	
11:00	p.m.	
12:00	a.m.	

Daily Plan for Sunday, May 31, 2015

12:00	a.m.	
1:00	a.m.	
2:00	a.m.	
3:00	a.m.	
4:00	a.m.	
5:00	a.m.	
6:00	a.m.	
7:00	a.m.	
8:00	a.m.	
9:00	a.m.	
10:00	a.m.	
11:00	a.m.	
12:00	p.m.	
1:00	p.m.	
2:00	p.m.	
3:00	p.m.	
4:00	p.m.	
5:00	p.m.	
6:00	p.m.	
7:00	p.m.	
8:00	p.m.	
9:00	p.m.	
10:00	p.m.	
11:00	p.m.	
12:00	a.m.	

Daily Plan for Monday, June 1, 2015

12:00	a.m.	
1:00	a.m.	
2:00	a.m.	
3:00	a.m.	
4:00	a.m.	
5:00	a.m.	
6:00	a.m.	
7:00	a.m.	
8:00	a.m.	
9:00	a.m.	
10:00	a.m.	
11:00	a.m.	
12:00	p.m.	
1:00	p.m.	
2:00	p.m.	
3:00	p.m.	
4:00	p.m.	
5:00	p.m.	
6:00	p.m.	
7:00	p.m.	
8:00	p.m.	
9:00	p.m.	
10:00	p.m.	
11:00	p.m.	
12:00	a.m.	

Daily Plan for Tuesday, June 2, 2015

12:00	a.m.	
1:00	a.m.	
2:00	a.m.	
3:00	a.m.	
4:00	a.m.	
5:00	a.m.	
6:00	a.m.	
7:00	a.m.	
8:00	a.m.	
9:00	a.m.	
10:00	a.m.	
11:00	a.m.	
12:00	p.m.	
1:00	p.m.	
2:00	p.m.	
3:00	p.m.	
4:00	p.m.	
5:00	p.m.	
6:00	p.m.	
7:00	p.m.	
8:00	p.m.	
9:00	p.m.	
10:00	p.m.	
11:00	p.m.	
12:00	a.m.	

Daily Plan for Wednesday, June 3, 2015

12:00	a.m.	
1:00	a.m.	
2:00	a.m.	
3:00	a.m.	
4:00	a.m.	
5:00	a.m.	
6:00	a.m.	
7:00	a.m.	
8:00	a.m.	
9:00	a.m.	
10:00	a.m.	
11:00	a.m.	
12:00	p.m.	
1:00	p.m.	
2:00	p.m.	
3:00	p.m.	
4:00	p.m.	
5:00	p.m.	
6:00	p.m.	
7:00	p.m.	
8:00	p.m.	
9:00	p.m.	
10:00	p.m.	
11:00	p.m.	
12:00	a.m.	

Daily Plan for Thursday, June 4, 2015

12:00	a.m.	
1:00	a.m.	
2:00	a.m.	
3:00	a.m.	
4:00	a.m.	
5:00	a.m.	
6:00	a.m.	
7:00	a.m.	
8:00	a.m.	
9:00	a.m.	
10:00	a.m.	
11:00	a.m.	
12:00	p.m.	
1:00	p.m.	
2:00	p.m.	
3:00	p.m.	
4:00	p.m.	
5:00	p.m.	
6:00	p.m.	
7:00	p.m.	
8:00	p.m.	
9:00	p.m.	
10:00	p.m.	
11:00	p.m.	
12:00	a.m.	

Daily Plan for Friday, June 5, 2015

12:00	a.m.	
1:00	a.m.	
2:00	a.m.	
3:00	a.m.	
4:00	a.m.	
5:00	a.m.	
6:00	a.m.	
7:00	a.m.	
8:00	a.m.	
9:00	a.m.	
10:00	a.m.	
11:00	a.m.	
12:00	p.m.	
1:00	p.m.	
2:00	p.m.	
3:00	p.m.	
4:00	p.m.	
5:00	p.m.	
6:00	p.m.	
7:00	p.m.	
8:00	p.m.	
9:00	p.m.	
10:00	p.m.	
11:00	p.m.	
12:00	a.m.	

Daily Plan for Saturday, June 6, 2015

12:00	a.m.	
1:00	a.m.	
2:00	a.m.	
3:00	a.m.	
4:00	a.m.	
5:00	a.m.	
6:00	a.m.	
7:00	a.m.	
8:00	a.m.	
9:00	a.m.	
10:00	a.m.	
11:00	a.m.	
12:00	p.m.	
1:00	p.m.	
2:00	p.m.	
3:00	p.m.	
4:00	p.m.	
5:00	p.m.	
6:00	p.m.	
7:00	p.m.	
8:00	p.m.	
9:00	p.m.	
10:00	p.m.	
11:00	p.m.	
12:00	a.m.	

Daily Plan for Sunday, June 7, 2015

12:00	a.m.	
1:00	a.m.	
2:00	a.m.	
3:00	a.m.	
4:00	a.m.	
5:00	a.m.	
6:00	a.m.	
7:00	a.m.	
8:00	a.m.	
9:00	a.m.	
10:00	a.m.	
11:00	a.m.	
12:00	p.m.	
1:00	p.m.	
2:00	p.m.	
3:00	p.m.	
4:00	p.m.	
5:00	p.m.	
6:00	p.m.	
7:00	p.m.	
8:00	p.m.	
9:00	p.m.	
10:00	p.m.	
11:00	p.m.	
12:00	a.m.	

Daily Plan for Monday, June 8, 2015

12:00	a.m.	
1:00	a.m.	
2:00	a.m.	
3:00	a.m.	
4:00	a.m.	
5:00	a.m.	
6:00	a.m.	
7:00	a.m.	
8:00	a.m.	
9:00	a.m.	
10:00	a.m.	
11:00	a.m.	
12:00	p.m.	
1:00	p.m.	
2:00	p.m.	
3:00	p.m.	
4:00	p.m.	
5:00	p.m.	
6:00	p.m.	
7:00	p.m.	
8:00	p.m.	
9:00	p.m.	
10:00	p.m.	
11:00	p.m.	
12:00	a.m.	

Daily Plan for Tuesday, June 9, 2015

12:00	a.m.	
1:00	a.m.	
2:00	a.m.	
3:00	a.m.	
4:00	a.m.	
5:00	a.m.	
6:00	a.m.	
7:00	a.m.	
8:00	a.m.	
9:00	a.m.	
10:00	a.m.	
11:00	a.m.	
12:00	p.m.	
1:00	p.m.	
2:00	p.m.	
3:00	p.m.	
4:00	p.m.	
5:00	p.m.	
6:00	p.m.	
7:00	p.m.	
8:00	p.m.	
9:00	p.m.	
10:00	p.m.	
11:00	p.m.	
12:00	a.m.	

Daily Plan for Wednesday, June 10, 2015

12:00	a.m.	
1:00	a.m.	
2:00	a.m.	
3:00	a.m.	
4:00	a.m.	
5:00	a.m.	
6:00	a.m.	
7:00	a.m.	
8:00	a.m.	
9:00	a.m.	
10:00	a.m.	
11:00	a.m.	
12:00	p.m.	
1:00	p.m.	
2:00	p.m.	
3:00	p.m.	
4:00	p.m.	
5:00	p.m.	
6:00	p.m.	
7:00	p.m.	
8:00	p.m.	
9:00	p.m.	
10:00	p.m.	
11:00	p.m.	
12:00	a.m.	

Daily Plan for Thursday, June 11, 2015

12:00	a.m.	
1:00	a.m.	
2:00	a.m.	
3:00	a.m.	
4:00	a.m.	
5:00	a.m.	
6:00	a.m.	
7:00	a.m.	
8:00	a.m.	
9:00	a.m.	
10:00	a.m.	
11:00	a.m.	
12:00	p.m.	
1:00	p.m.	
2:00	p.m.	
3:00	p.m.	
4:00	p.m.	
5:00	p.m.	
6:00	p.m.	
7:00	p.m.	
8:00	p.m.	
9:00	p.m.	
10:00	p.m.	
11:00	p.m.	
12:00	a.m.	

Daily Plan for Friday, June 12, 2015

12:00	a.m.	
1:00	a.m.	
2:00	a.m.	
3:00	a.m.	
4:00	a.m.	
5:00	a.m.	
6:00	a.m.	
7:00	a.m.	
8:00	a.m.	
9:00	a.m.	
10:00	a.m.	
11:00	a.m.	
12:00	p.m.	
1:00	p.m.	
2:00	p.m.	
3:00	p.m.	
4:00	p.m.	
5:00	p.m.	
6:00	p.m.	
7:00	p.m.	
8:00	p.m.	
9:00	p.m.	
10:00	p.m.	
11:00	p.m.	
12:00	a.m.	

Daily Plan for Saturday, June 13, 2015

12:00	a.m.	
1:00	a.m.	
2:00	a.m.	
3:00	a.m.	
4:00	a.m.	
5:00	a.m.	
6:00	a.m.	
7:00	a.m.	
8:00	a.m.	
9:00	a.m.	
10:00	a.m.	
11:00	a.m.	
12:00	p.m.	
1:00	p.m.	
2:00	p.m.	
3:00	p.m.	
4:00	p.m.	
5:00	p.m.	
6:00	p.m.	
7:00	p.m.	
8:00	p.m.	
9:00	p.m.	
10:00	p.m.	
11:00	p.m.	
12:00	a.m.	

Daily Plan for Sunday, June 14, 2015

12:00	a.m.	
1:00	a.m.	
2:00	a.m.	
3:00	a.m.	
4:00	a.m.	
5:00	a.m.	
6:00	a.m.	
7:00	a.m.	
8:00	a.m.	
9:00	a.m.	
10:00	a.m.	
11:00	a.m.	
12:00	p.m.	
1:00	p.m.	
2:00	p.m.	
3:00	p.m.	
4:00	p.m.	
5:00	p.m.	
6:00	p.m.	
7:00	p.m.	
8:00	p.m.	
9:00	p.m.	
10:00	p.m.	
11:00	p.m.	
12:00	a.m.	

Daily Plan for Monday, June 15, 2015

12:00	a.m.	
1:00	a.m.	
2:00	a.m.	
3:00	a.m.	
4:00	a.m.	
5:00	a.m.	
6:00	a.m.	
7:00	a.m.	
8:00	a.m.	
9:00	a.m.	
10:00	a.m.	
11:00	a.m.	
12:00	p.m.	
1:00	p.m.	
2:00	p.m.	
3:00	p.m.	
4:00	p.m.	
5:00	p.m.	
6:00	p.m.	
7:00	p.m.	
8:00	p.m.	
9:00	p.m.	
10:00	p.m.	
11:00	p.m.	
12:00	a.m.	

Daily Plan for Tuesday, June 16, 2015

Time	
12:00 a.m.	
1:00 a.m.	
2:00 a.m.	
3:00 a.m.	
4:00 a.m.	
5:00 a.m.	
6:00 a.m.	
7:00 a.m.	
8:00 a.m.	
9:00 a.m.	
10:00 a.m.	
11:00 a.m.	
12:00 p.m.	
1:00 p.m.	
2:00 p.m.	
3:00 p.m.	
4:00 p.m.	
5:00 p.m.	
6:00 p.m.	
7:00 p.m.	
8:00 p.m.	
9:00 p.m.	
10:00 p.m.	
11:00 p.m.	
12:00 a.m.	

Daily Plan for Wednesday, June 17, 2015

12:00	a.m.	
1:00	a.m.	
2:00	a.m.	
3:00	a.m.	
4:00	a.m.	
5:00	a.m.	
6:00	a.m.	
7:00	a.m.	
8:00	a.m.	
9:00	a.m.	
10:00	a.m.	
11:00	a.m.	
12:00	p.m.	
1:00	p.m.	
2:00	p.m.	
3:00	p.m.	
4:00	p.m.	
5:00	p.m.	
6:00	p.m.	
7:00	p.m.	
8:00	p.m.	
9:00	p.m.	
10:00	p.m.	
11:00	p.m.	
12:00	a.m.	

Daily Plan for Thursday, June 18, 2015

12:00	a.m.	
1:00	a.m.	
2:00	a.m.	
3:00	a.m.	
4:00	a.m.	
5:00	a.m.	
6:00	a.m.	
7:00	a.m.	
8:00	a.m.	
9:00	a.m.	
10:00	a.m.	
11:00	a.m.	
12:00	p.m.	
1:00	p.m.	
2:00	p.m.	
3:00	p.m.	
4:00	p.m.	
5:00	p.m.	
6:00	p.m.	
7:00	p.m.	
8:00	p.m.	
9:00	p.m.	
10:00	p.m.	
11:00	p.m.	
12:00	a.m.	

Daily Plan for Friday, June 19, 2015

12:00	a.m.	
1:00	a.m.	
2:00	a.m.	
3:00	a.m.	
4:00	a.m.	
5:00	a.m.	
6:00	a.m.	
7:00	a.m.	
8:00	a.m.	
9:00	a.m.	
10:00	a.m.	
11:00	a.m.	
12:00	p.m.	
1:00	p.m.	
2:00	p.m.	
3:00	p.m.	
4:00	p.m.	
5:00	p.m.	
6:00	p.m.	
7:00	p.m.	
8:00	p.m.	
9:00	p.m.	
10:00	p.m.	
11:00	p.m.	
12:00	a.m.	

Daily Plan for Saturday, June 20, 2015

12:00	a.m.	
1:00	a.m.	
2:00	a.m.	
3:00	a.m.	
4:00	a.m.	
5:00	a.m.	
6:00	a.m.	
7:00	a.m.	
8:00	a.m.	
9:00	a.m.	
10:00	a.m.	
11:00	a.m.	
12:00	p.m.	
1:00	p.m.	
2:00	p.m.	
3:00	p.m.	
4:00	p.m.	
5:00	p.m.	
6:00	p.m.	
7:00	p.m.	
8:00	p.m.	
9:00	p.m.	
10:00	p.m.	
11:00	p.m.	
12:00	a.m.	

Daily Plan for Sunday, June 21, 2015

12:00	a.m.	
1:00	a.m.	
2:00	a.m.	
3:00	a.m.	
4:00	a.m.	
5:00	a.m.	
6:00	a.m.	
7:00	a.m.	
8:00	a.m.	
9:00	a.m.	
10:00	a.m.	
11:00	a.m.	
12:00	p.m.	
1:00	p.m.	
2:00	p.m.	
3:00	p.m.	
4:00	p.m.	
5:00	p.m.	
6:00	p.m.	
7:00	p.m.	
8:00	p.m.	
9:00	p.m.	
10:00	p.m.	
11:00	p.m.	
12:00	a.m.	

Daily Plan for Monday, June 22, 2015

12:00	a.m.	
1:00	a.m.	
2:00	a.m.	
3:00	a.m.	
4:00	a.m.	
5:00	a.m.	
6:00	a.m.	
7:00	a.m.	
8:00	a.m.	
9:00	a.m.	
10:00	a.m.	
11:00	a.m.	
12:00	p.m.	
1:00	p.m.	
2:00	p.m.	
3:00	p.m.	
4:00	p.m.	
5:00	p.m.	
6:00	p.m.	
7:00	p.m.	
8:00	p.m.	
9:00	p.m.	
10:00	p.m.	
11:00	p.m.	
12:00	a.m.	

Daily Plan for Tuesday, June 23, 2015

12:00	a.m.	
1:00	a.m.	
2:00	a.m.	
3:00	a.m.	
4:00	a.m.	
5:00	a.m.	
6:00	a.m.	
7:00	a.m.	
8:00	a.m.	
9:00	a.m.	
10:00	a.m.	
11:00	a.m.	
12:00	p.m.	
1:00	p.m.	
2:00	p.m.	
3:00	p.m.	
4:00	p.m.	
5:00	p.m.	
6:00	p.m.	
7:00	p.m.	
8:00	p.m.	
9:00	p.m.	
10:00	p.m.	
11:00	p.m.	
12:00	a.m.	

Daily Plan for Wednesday, June 24, 2015

12:00	a.m.	
1:00	a.m.	
2:00	a.m.	
3:00	a.m.	
4:00	a.m.	
5:00	a.m.	
6:00	a.m.	
7:00	a.m.	
8:00	a.m.	
9:00	a.m.	
10:00	a.m.	
11:00	a.m.	
12:00	p.m.	
1:00	p.m.	
2:00	p.m.	
3:00	p.m.	
4:00	p.m.	
5:00	p.m.	
6:00	p.m.	
7:00	p.m.	
8:00	p.m.	
9:00	p.m.	
10:00	p.m.	
11:00	p.m.	
12:00	a.m.	

Daily Plan for Thursday, June 25, 2015

12:00	a.m.	
1:00	a.m.	
2:00	a.m.	
3:00	a.m.	
4:00	a.m.	
5:00	a.m.	
6:00	a.m.	
7:00	a.m.	
8:00	a.m.	
9:00	a.m.	
10:00	a.m.	
11:00	a.m.	
12:00	p.m.	
1:00	p.m.	
2:00	p.m.	
3:00	p.m.	
4:00	p.m.	
5:00	p.m.	
6:00	p.m.	
7:00	p.m.	
8:00	p.m.	
9:00	p.m.	
10:00	p.m.	
11:00	p.m.	
12:00	a.m.	

Daily Plan for Friday, June 26, 2015

12:00	a.m.	
1:00	a.m.	
2:00	a.m.	
3:00	a.m.	
4:00	a.m.	
5:00	a.m.	
6:00	a.m.	
7:00	a.m.	
8:00	a.m.	
9:00	a.m.	
10:00	a.m.	
11:00	a.m.	
12:00	p.m.	
1:00	p.m.	
2:00	p.m.	
3:00	p.m.	
4:00	p.m.	
5:00	p.m.	
6:00	p.m.	
7:00	p.m.	
8:00	p.m.	
9:00	p.m.	
10:00	p.m.	
11:00	p.m.	
12:00	a.m.	

Daily Plan for Saturday, June 27, 2015

12:00	a.m.	
1:00	a.m.	
2:00	a.m.	
3:00	a.m.	
4:00	a.m.	
5:00	a.m.	
6:00	a.m.	
7:00	a.m.	
8:00	a.m.	
9:00	a.m.	
10:00	a.m.	
11:00	a.m.	
12:00	p.m.	
1:00	p.m.	
2:00	p.m.	
3:00	p.m.	
4:00	p.m.	
5:00	p.m.	
6:00	p.m.	
7:00	p.m.	
8:00	p.m.	
9:00	p.m.	
10:00	p.m.	
11:00	p.m.	
12:00	a.m.	

Daily Plan for Sunday, June 28, 2015

12:00	a.m.	
1:00	a.m.	
2:00	a.m.	
3:00	a.m.	
4:00	a.m.	
5:00	a.m.	
6:00	a.m.	
7:00	a.m.	
8:00	a.m.	
9:00	a.m.	
10:00	a.m.	
11:00	a.m.	
12:00	p.m.	
1:00	p.m.	
2:00	p.m.	
3:00	p.m.	
4:00	p.m.	
5:00	p.m.	
6:00	p.m.	
7:00	p.m.	
8:00	p.m.	
9:00	p.m.	
10:00	p.m.	
11:00	p.m.	
12:00	a.m.	

Daily Plan for Monday, June 29, 2015

12:00	a.m.	
1:00	a.m.	
2:00	a.m.	
3:00	a.m.	
4:00	a.m.	
5:00	a.m.	
6:00	a.m.	
7:00	a.m.	
8:00	a.m.	
9:00	a.m.	
10:00	a.m.	
11:00	a.m.	
12:00	p.m.	
1:00	p.m.	
2:00	p.m.	
3:00	p.m.	
4:00	p.m.	
5:00	p.m.	
6:00	p.m.	
7:00	p.m.	
8:00	p.m.	
9:00	p.m.	
10:00	p.m.	
11:00	p.m.	
12:00	a.m.	

Daily Plan for Tuesday, June 30, 2015

12:00	a.m.	
1:00	a.m.	
2:00	a.m.	
3:00	a.m.	
4:00	a.m.	
5:00	a.m.	
6:00	a.m.	
7:00	a.m.	
8:00	a.m.	
9:00	a.m.	
10:00	a.m.	
11:00	a.m.	
12:00	p.m.	
1:00	p.m.	
2:00	p.m.	
3:00	p.m.	
4:00	p.m.	
5:00	p.m.	
6:00	p.m.	
7:00	p.m.	
8:00	p.m.	
9:00	p.m.	
10:00	p.m.	
11:00	p.m.	
12:00	a.m.	

Daily Plan for Wednesday, July 1, 2015

12:00	a.m.	
1:00	a.m.	
2:00	a.m.	
3:00	a.m.	
4:00	a.m.	
5:00	a.m.	
6:00	a.m.	
7:00	a.m.	
8:00	a.m.	
9:00	a.m.	
10:00	a.m.	
11:00	a.m.	
12:00	p.m.	
1:00	p.m.	
2:00	p.m.	
3:00	p.m.	
4:00	p.m.	
5:00	p.m.	
6:00	p.m.	
7:00	p.m.	
8:00	p.m.	
9:00	p.m.	
10:00	p.m.	
11:00	p.m.	
12:00	a.m.	

Daily Plan for Thursday, July 2, 2015

12:00	a.m.	
1:00	a.m.	
2:00	a.m.	
3:00	a.m.	
4:00	a.m.	
5:00	a.m.	
6:00	a.m.	
7:00	a.m.	
8:00	a.m.	
9:00	a.m.	
10:00	a.m.	
11:00	a.m.	
12:00	p.m.	
1:00	p.m.	
2:00	p.m.	
3:00	p.m.	
4:00	p.m.	
5:00	p.m.	
6:00	p.m.	
7:00	p.m.	
8:00	p.m.	
9:00	p.m.	
10:00	p.m.	
11:00	p.m.	
12:00	a.m.	

Daily Plan for Friday, July 3, 2015

12:00	a.m.	
1:00	a.m.	
2:00	a.m.	
3:00	a.m.	
4:00	a.m.	
5:00	a.m.	
6:00	a.m.	
7:00	a.m.	
8:00	a.m.	
9:00	a.m.	
10:00	a.m.	
11:00	a.m.	
12:00	p.m.	
1:00	p.m.	
2:00	p.m.	
3:00	p.m.	
4:00	p.m.	
5:00	p.m.	
6:00	p.m.	
7:00	p.m.	
8:00	p.m.	
9:00	p.m.	
10:00	p.m.	
11:00	p.m.	
12:00	a.m.	

Daily Plan for Saturday, July 4, 2015

12:00	a.m.	
1:00	a.m.	
2:00	a.m.	
3:00	a.m.	
4:00	a.m.	
5:00	a.m.	
6:00	a.m.	
7:00	a.m.	
8:00	a.m.	
9:00	a.m.	
10:00	a.m.	
11:00	a.m.	
12:00	p.m.	
1:00	p.m.	
2:00	p.m.	
3:00	p.m.	
4:00	p.m.	
5:00	p.m.	
6:00	p.m.	
7:00	p.m.	
8:00	p.m.	
9:00	p.m.	
10:00	p.m.	
11:00	p.m.	
12:00	a.m.	

Daily Plan for Sunday, July 5, 2015

12:00	a.m.	
1:00	a.m.	
2:00	a.m.	
3:00	a.m.	
4:00	a.m.	
5:00	a.m.	
6:00	a.m.	
7:00	a.m.	
8:00	a.m.	
9:00	a.m.	
10:00	a.m.	
11:00	a.m.	
12:00	p.m.	
1:00	p.m.	
2:00	p.m.	
3:00	p.m.	
4:00	p.m.	
5:00	p.m.	
6:00	p.m.	
7:00	p.m.	
8:00	p.m.	
9:00	p.m.	
10:00	p.m.	
11:00	p.m.	
12:00	a.m.	

Daily Plan for Monday, July 6, 2015

12:00	a.m.	
1:00	a.m.	
2:00	a.m.	
3:00	a.m.	
4:00	a.m.	
5:00	a.m.	
6:00	a.m.	
7:00	a.m.	
8:00	a.m.	
9:00	a.m.	
10:00	a.m.	
11:00	a.m.	
12:00	p.m.	
1:00	p.m.	
2:00	p.m.	
3:00	p.m.	
4:00	p.m.	
5:00	p.m.	
6:00	p.m.	
7:00	p.m.	
8:00	p.m.	
9:00	p.m.	
10:00	p.m.	
11:00	p.m.	
12:00	a.m.	

Daily Plan for Tuesday, July 7, 2015

12:00 a.m.	
1:00 a.m.	
2:00 a.m.	
3:00 a.m.	
4:00 a.m.	
5:00 a.m.	
6:00 a.m.	
7:00 a.m.	
8:00 a.m.	
9:00 a.m.	
10:00 a.m.	
11:00 a.m.	
12:00 p.m.	
1:00 p.m.	
2:00 p.m.	
3:00 p.m.	
4:00 p.m.	
5:00 p.m.	
6:00 p.m.	
7:00 p.m.	
8:00 p.m.	
9:00 p.m.	
10:00 p.m.	
11:00 p.m.	
12:00 a.m.	

Daily Plan for Wednesday, July 8, 2015

12:00	a.m.	
1:00	a.m.	
2:00	a.m.	
3:00	a.m.	
4:00	a.m.	
5:00	a.m.	
6:00	a.m.	
7:00	a.m.	
8:00	a.m.	
9:00	a.m.	
10:00	a.m.	
11:00	a.m.	
12:00	p.m.	
1:00	p.m.	
2:00	p.m.	
3:00	p.m.	
4:00	p.m.	
5:00	p.m.	
6:00	p.m.	
7:00	p.m.	
8:00	p.m.	
9:00	p.m.	
10:00	p.m.	
11:00	p.m.	
12:00	a.m.	

Daily Plan for Thursday, July 9, 2015

12:00	a.m.	
1:00	a.m.	
2:00	a.m.	
3:00	a.m.	
4:00	a.m.	
5:00	a.m.	
6:00	a.m.	
7:00	a.m.	
8:00	a.m.	
9:00	a.m.	
10:00	a.m.	
11:00	a.m.	
12:00	p.m.	
1:00	p.m.	
2:00	p.m.	
3:00	p.m.	
4:00	p.m.	
5:00	p.m.	
6:00	p.m.	
7:00	p.m.	
8:00	p.m.	
9:00	p.m.	
10:00	p.m.	
11:00	p.m.	
12:00	a.m.	

Daily Plan for Friday, July 10, 2015

12:00	a.m.	
1:00	a.m.	
2:00	a.m.	
3:00	a.m.	
4:00	a.m.	
5:00	a.m.	
6:00	a.m.	
7:00	a.m.	
8:00	a.m.	
9:00	a.m.	
10:00	a.m.	
11:00	a.m.	
12:00	p.m.	
1:00	p.m.	
2:00	p.m.	
3:00	p.m.	
4:00	p.m.	
5:00	p.m.	
6:00	p.m.	
7:00	p.m.	
8:00	p.m.	
9:00	p.m.	
10:00	p.m.	
11:00	p.m.	
12:00	a.m.	

Daily Plan for Saturday, July 11, 2015

Time	
12:00	a.m.
1:00	a.m.
2:00	a.m.
3:00	a.m.
4:00	a.m.
5:00	a.m.
6:00	a.m.
7:00	a.m.
8:00	a.m.
9:00	a.m.
10:00	a.m.
11:00	a.m.
12:00	p.m.
1:00	p.m.
2:00	p.m.
3:00	p.m.
4:00	p.m.
5:00	p.m.
6:00	p.m.
7:00	p.m.
8:00	p.m.
9:00	p.m.
10:00	p.m.
11:00	p.m.
12:00	a.m.

Daily Plan for Sunday, July 12, 2015

12:00	a.m.	
1:00	a.m.	
2:00	a.m.	
3:00	a.m.	
4:00	a.m.	
5:00	a.m.	
6:00	a.m.	
7:00	a.m.	
8:00	a.m.	
9:00	a.m.	
10:00	a.m.	
11:00	a.m.	
12:00	p.m.	
1:00	p.m.	
2:00	p.m.	
3:00	p.m.	
4:00	p.m.	
5:00	p.m.	
6:00	p.m.	
7:00	p.m.	
8:00	p.m.	
9:00	p.m.	
10:00	p.m.	
11:00	p.m.	
12:00	a.m.	

Daily Plan for Monday, July 13, 2015

12:00	a.m.	
1:00	a.m.	
2:00	a.m.	
3:00	a.m.	
4:00	a.m.	
5:00	a.m.	
6:00	a.m.	
7:00	a.m.	
8:00	a.m.	
9:00	a.m.	
10:00	a.m.	
11:00	a.m.	
12:00	p.m.	
1:00	p.m.	
2:00	p.m.	
3:00	p.m.	
4:00	p.m.	
5:00	p.m.	
6:00	p.m.	
7:00	p.m.	
8:00	p.m.	
9:00	p.m.	
10:00	p.m.	
11:00	p.m.	
12:00	a.m.	

Daily Plan for Tuesday, July 14, 2015

Time		
12:00	a.m.	
1:00	a.m.	
2:00	a.m.	
3:00	a.m.	
4:00	a.m.	
5:00	a.m.	
6:00	a.m.	
7:00	a.m.	
8:00	a.m.	
9:00	a.m.	
10:00	a.m.	
11:00	a.m.	
12:00	p.m.	
1:00	p.m.	
2:00	p.m.	
3:00	p.m.	
4:00	p.m.	
5:00	p.m.	
6:00	p.m.	
7:00	p.m.	
8:00	p.m.	
9:00	p.m.	
10:00	p.m.	
11:00	p.m.	
12:00	a.m.	

Daily Plan for Wednesday, July 15, 2015

Time		
12:00	a.m.	
1:00	a.m.	
2:00	a.m.	
3:00	a.m.	
4:00	a.m.	
5:00	a.m.	
6:00	a.m.	
7:00	a.m.	
8:00	a.m.	
9:00	a.m.	
10:00	a.m.	
11:00	a.m.	
12:00	p.m.	
1:00	p.m.	
2:00	p.m.	
3:00	p.m.	
4:00	p.m.	
5:00	p.m.	
6:00	p.m.	
7:00	p.m.	
8:00	p.m.	
9:00	p.m.	
10:00	p.m.	
11:00	p.m.	
12:00	a.m.	

Daily Plan for Thursday, July 16, 2015

12:00	a.m.	
1:00	a.m.	
2:00	a.m.	
3:00	a.m.	
4:00	a.m.	
5:00	a.m.	
6:00	a.m.	
7:00	a.m.	
8:00	a.m.	
9:00	a.m.	
10:00	a.m.	
11:00	a.m.	
12:00	p.m.	
1:00	p.m.	
2:00	p.m.	
3:00	p.m.	
4:00	p.m.	
5:00	p.m.	
6:00	p.m.	
7:00	p.m.	
8:00	p.m.	
9:00	p.m.	
10:00	p.m.	
11:00	p.m.	
12:00	a.m.	

Daily Plan for Friday, July 17, 2015

12:00	a.m.	
1:00	a.m.	
2:00	a.m.	
3:00	a.m.	
4:00	a.m.	
5:00	a.m.	
6:00	a.m.	
7:00	a.m.	
8:00	a.m.	
9:00	a.m.	
10:00	a.m.	
11:00	a.m.	
12:00	p.m.	
1:00	p.m.	
2:00	p.m.	
3:00	p.m.	
4:00	p.m.	
5:00	p.m.	
6:00	p.m.	
7:00	p.m.	
8:00	p.m.	
9:00	p.m.	
10:00	p.m.	
11:00	p.m.	
12:00	a.m.	

Daily Plan for Saturday, July 18, 2015

12:00	a.m.	
1:00	a.m.	
2:00	a.m.	
3:00	a.m.	
4:00	a.m.	
5:00	a.m.	
6:00	a.m.	
7:00	a.m.	
8:00	a.m.	
9:00	a.m.	
10:00	a.m.	
11:00	a.m.	
12:00	p.m.	
1:00	p.m.	
2:00	p.m.	
3:00	p.m.	
4:00	p.m.	
5:00	p.m.	
6:00	p.m.	
7:00	p.m.	
8:00	p.m.	
9:00	p.m.	
10:00	p.m.	
11:00	p.m.	
12:00	a.m.	

Daily Plan for Sunday, July 19, 2015

12:00	a.m.	
1:00	a.m.	
2:00	a.m.	
3:00	a.m.	
4:00	a.m.	
5:00	a.m.	
6:00	a.m.	
7:00	a.m.	
8:00	a.m.	
9:00	a.m.	
10:00	a.m.	
11:00	a.m.	
12:00	p.m.	
1:00	p.m.	
2:00	p.m.	
3:00	p.m.	
4:00	p.m.	
5:00	p.m.	
6:00	p.m.	
7:00	p.m.	
8:00	p.m.	
9:00	p.m.	
10:00	p.m.	
11:00	p.m.	
12:00	a.m.	

Daily Plan for Monday, July 20, 2015

12:00	a.m.	
1:00	a.m.	
2:00	a.m.	
3:00	a.m.	
4:00	a.m.	
5:00	a.m.	
6:00	a.m.	
7:00	a.m.	
8:00	a.m.	
9:00	a.m.	
10:00	a.m.	
11:00	a.m.	
12:00	p.m.	
1:00	p.m.	
2:00	p.m.	
3:00	p.m.	
4:00	p.m.	
5:00	p.m.	
6:00	p.m.	
7:00	p.m.	
8:00	p.m.	
9:00	p.m.	
10:00	p.m.	
11:00	p.m.	
12:00	a.m.	

Daily Plan for Tuesday, July 21, 2015

12:00	a.m.	
1:00	a.m.	
2:00	a.m.	
3:00	a.m.	
4:00	a.m.	
5:00	a.m.	
6:00	a.m.	
7:00	a.m.	
8:00	a.m.	
9:00	a.m.	
10:00	a.m.	
11:00	a.m.	
12:00	p.m.	
1:00	p.m.	
2:00	p.m.	
3:00	p.m.	
4:00	p.m.	
5:00	p.m.	
6:00	p.m.	
7:00	p.m.	
8:00	p.m.	
9:00	p.m.	
10:00	p.m.	
11:00	p.m.	
12:00	a.m.	

Daily Plan for Wednesday, July 22, 2015

Time		
12:00	a.m.	
1:00	a.m.	
2:00	a.m.	
3:00	a.m.	
4:00	a.m.	
5:00	a.m.	
6:00	a.m.	
7:00	a.m.	
8:00	a.m.	
9:00	a.m.	
10:00	a.m.	
11:00	a.m.	
12:00	p.m.	
1:00	p.m.	
2:00	p.m.	
3:00	p.m.	
4:00	p.m.	
5:00	p.m.	
6:00	p.m.	
7:00	p.m.	
8:00	p.m.	
9:00	p.m.	
10:00	p.m.	
11:00	p.m.	
12:00	a.m.	

Daily Plan for Thursday, July 23, 2015

12:00	a.m.	
1:00	a.m.	
2:00	a.m.	
3:00	a.m.	
4:00	a.m.	
5:00	a.m.	
6:00	a.m.	
7:00	a.m.	
8:00	a.m.	
9:00	a.m.	
10:00	a.m.	
11:00	a.m.	
12:00	p.m.	
1:00	p.m.	
2:00	p.m.	
3:00	p.m.	
4:00	p.m.	
5:00	p.m.	
6:00	p.m.	
7:00	p.m.	
8:00	p.m.	
9:00	p.m.	
10:00	p.m.	
11:00	p.m.	
12:00	a.m.	

Daily Plan for Friday, July 24, 2015

12:00	a.m.	
1:00	a.m.	
2:00	a.m.	
3:00	a.m.	
4:00	a.m.	
5:00	a.m.	
6:00	a.m.	
7:00	a.m.	
8:00	a.m.	
9:00	a.m.	
10:00	a.m.	
11:00	a.m.	
12:00	p.m.	
1:00	p.m.	
2:00	p.m.	
3:00	p.m.	
4:00	p.m.	
5:00	p.m.	
6:00	p.m.	
7:00	p.m.	
8:00	p.m.	
9:00	p.m.	
10:00	p.m.	
11:00	p.m.	
12:00	a.m.	

Daily Plan for Saturday, July 25, 2015

12:00	a.m.	
1:00	a.m.	
2:00	a.m.	
3:00	a.m.	
4:00	a.m.	
5:00	a.m.	
6:00	a.m.	
7:00	a.m.	
8:00	a.m.	
9:00	a.m.	
10:00	a.m.	
11:00	a.m.	
12:00	p.m.	
1:00	p.m.	
2:00	p.m.	
3:00	p.m.	
4:00	p.m.	
5:00	p.m.	
6:00	p.m.	
7:00	p.m.	
8:00	p.m.	
9:00	p.m.	
10:00	p.m.	
11:00	p.m.	
12:00	a.m.	

Daily Plan for Sunday, July 26, 2015

12:00	a.m.	
1:00	a.m.	
2:00	a.m.	
3:00	a.m.	
4:00	a.m.	
5:00	a.m.	
6:00	a.m.	
7:00	a.m.	
8:00	a.m.	
9:00	a.m.	
10:00	a.m.	
11:00	a.m.	
12:00	p.m.	
1:00	p.m.	
2:00	p.m.	
3:00	p.m.	
4:00	p.m.	
5:00	p.m.	
6:00	p.m.	
7:00	p.m.	
8:00	p.m.	
9:00	p.m.	
10:00	p.m.	
11:00	p.m.	
12:00	a.m.	

Daily Plan for Monday, July 27, 2015

12:00	a.m.	
1:00	a.m.	
2:00	a.m.	
3:00	a.m.	
4:00	a.m.	
5:00	a.m.	
6:00	a.m.	
7:00	a.m.	
8:00	a.m.	
9:00	a.m.	
10:00	a.m.	
11:00	a.m.	
12:00	p.m.	
1:00	p.m.	
2:00	p.m.	
3:00	p.m.	
4:00	p.m.	
5:00	p.m.	
6:00	p.m.	
7:00	p.m.	
8:00	p.m.	
9:00	p.m.	
10:00	p.m.	
11:00	p.m.	
12:00	a.m.	

Daily Plan for Tuesday, July 28, 2015

12:00	a.m.	
1:00	a.m.	
2:00	a.m.	
3:00	a.m.	
4:00	a.m.	
5:00	a.m.	
6:00	a.m.	
7:00	a.m.	
8:00	a.m.	
9:00	a.m.	
10:00	a.m.	
11:00	a.m.	
12:00	p.m.	
1:00	p.m.	
2:00	p.m.	
3:00	p.m.	
4:00	p.m.	
5:00	p.m.	
6:00	p.m.	
7:00	p.m.	
8:00	p.m.	
9:00	p.m.	
10:00	p.m.	
11:00	p.m.	
12:00	a.m.	

Daily Plan for Wednesday, July 29, 2015

Time		
12:00	a.m.	
1:00	a.m.	
2:00	a.m.	
3:00	a.m.	
4:00	a.m.	
5:00	a.m.	
6:00	a.m.	
7:00	a.m.	
8:00	a.m.	
9:00	a.m.	
10:00	a.m.	
11:00	a.m.	
12:00	p.m.	
1:00	p.m.	
2:00	p.m.	
3:00	p.m.	
4:00	p.m.	
5:00	p.m.	
6:00	p.m.	
7:00	p.m.	
8:00	p.m.	
9:00	p.m.	
10:00	p.m.	
11:00	p.m.	
12:00	a.m.	

Daily Plan for Thursday, July 30, 2015

12:00	a.m.	
1:00	a.m.	
2:00	a.m.	
3:00	a.m.	
4:00	a.m.	
5:00	a.m.	
6:00	a.m.	
7:00	a.m.	
8:00	a.m.	
9:00	a.m.	
10:00	a.m.	
11:00	a.m.	
12:00	p.m.	
1:00	p.m.	
2:00	p.m.	
3:00	p.m.	
4:00	p.m.	
5:00	p.m.	
6:00	p.m.	
7:00	p.m.	
8:00	p.m.	
9:00	p.m.	
10:00	p.m.	
11:00	p.m.	
12:00	a.m.	

Daily Plan for Friday, July 31, 2015

12:00	a.m.	
1:00	a.m.	
2:00	a.m.	
3:00	a.m.	
4:00	a.m.	
5:00	a.m.	
6:00	a.m.	
7:00	a.m.	
8:00	a.m.	
9:00	a.m.	
10:00	a.m.	
11:00	a.m.	
12:00	p.m.	
1:00	p.m.	
2:00	p.m.	
3:00	p.m.	
4:00	p.m.	
5:00	p.m.	
6:00	p.m.	
7:00	p.m.	
8:00	p.m.	
9:00	p.m.	
10:00	p.m.	
11:00	p.m.	
12:00	a.m.	

Daily Plan for Saturday, August 1, 2015

Time		
12:00	a.m.	
1:00	a.m.	
2:00	a.m.	
3:00	a.m.	
4:00	a.m.	
5:00	a.m.	
6:00	a.m.	
7:00	a.m.	
8:00	a.m.	
9:00	a.m.	
10:00	a.m.	
11:00	a.m.	
12:00	p.m.	
1:00	p.m.	
2:00	p.m.	
3:00	p.m.	
4:00	p.m.	
5:00	p.m.	
6:00	p.m.	
7:00	p.m.	
8:00	p.m.	
9:00	p.m.	
10:00	p.m.	
11:00	p.m.	
12:00	a.m.	

Daily Plan for Sunday, August 2, 2015

Time		
12:00	a.m.	
1:00	a.m.	
2:00	a.m.	
3:00	a.m.	
4:00	a.m.	
5:00	a.m.	
6:00	a.m.	
7:00	a.m.	
8:00	a.m.	
9:00	a.m.	
10:00	a.m.	
11:00	a.m.	
12:00	p.m.	
1:00	p.m.	
2:00	p.m.	
3:00	p.m.	
4:00	p.m.	
5:00	p.m.	
6:00	p.m.	
7:00	p.m.	
8:00	p.m.	
9:00	p.m.	
10:00	p.m.	
11:00	p.m.	
12:00	a.m.	

Daily Plan for Monday, August 3, 2015

12:00	a.m.	
1:00	a.m.	
2:00	a.m.	
3:00	a.m.	
4:00	a.m.	
5:00	a.m.	
6:00	a.m.	
7:00	a.m.	
8:00	a.m.	
9:00	a.m.	
10:00	a.m.	
11:00	a.m.	
12:00	p.m.	
1:00	p.m.	
2:00	p.m.	
3:00	p.m.	
4:00	p.m.	
5:00	p.m.	
6:00	p.m.	
7:00	p.m.	
8:00	p.m.	
9:00	p.m.	
10:00	p.m.	
11:00	p.m.	
12:00	a.m.	

Daily Plan for Tuesday, August 4, 2015

12:00	a.m.	
1:00	a.m.	
2:00	a.m.	
3:00	a.m.	
4:00	a.m.	
5:00	a.m.	
6:00	a.m.	
7:00	a.m.	
8:00	a.m.	
9:00	a.m.	
10:00	a.m.	
11:00	a.m.	
12:00	p.m.	
1:00	p.m.	
2:00	p.m.	
3:00	p.m.	
4:00	p.m.	
5:00	p.m.	
6:00	p.m.	
7:00	p.m.	
8:00	p.m.	
9:00	p.m.	
10:00	p.m.	
11:00	p.m.	
12:00	a.m.	

Daily Plan for Wednesday, August 5, 2015

12:00	a.m.	
1:00	a.m.	
2:00	a.m.	
3:00	a.m.	
4:00	a.m.	
5:00	a.m.	
6:00	a.m.	
7:00	a.m.	
8:00	a.m.	
9:00	a.m.	
10:00	a.m.	
11:00	a.m.	
12:00	p.m.	
1:00	p.m.	
2:00	p.m.	
3:00	p.m.	
4:00	p.m.	
5:00	p.m.	
6:00	p.m.	
7:00	p.m.	
8:00	p.m.	
9:00	p.m.	
10:00	p.m.	
11:00	p.m.	
12:00	a.m.	

Daily Plan for Thursday, August 6, 2015

12:00	a.m.	
1:00	a.m.	
2:00	a.m.	
3:00	a.m.	
4:00	a.m.	
5:00	a.m.	
6:00	a.m.	
7:00	a.m.	
8:00	a.m.	
9:00	a.m.	
10:00	a.m.	
11:00	a.m.	
12:00	p.m.	
1:00	p.m.	
2:00	p.m.	
3:00	p.m.	
4:00	p.m.	
5:00	p.m.	
6:00	p.m.	
7:00	p.m.	
8:00	p.m.	
9:00	p.m.	
10:00	p.m.	
11:00	p.m.	
12:00	a.m.	

Daily Plan for Friday, August 7, 2015

12:00	a.m.	
1:00	a.m.	
2:00	a.m.	
3:00	a.m.	
4:00	a.m.	
5:00	a.m.	
6:00	a.m.	
7:00	a.m.	
8:00	a.m.	
9:00	a.m.	
10:00	a.m.	
11:00	a.m.	
12:00	p.m.	
1:00	p.m.	
2:00	p.m.	
3:00	p.m.	
4:00	p.m.	
5:00	p.m.	
6:00	p.m.	
7:00	p.m.	
8:00	p.m.	
9:00	p.m.	
10:00	p.m.	
11:00	p.m.	
12:00	a.m.	

Daily Plan for Saturday, August 8, 2015

Time		
12:00	a.m.	
1:00	a.m.	
2:00	a.m.	
3:00	a.m.	
4:00	a.m.	
5:00	a.m.	
6:00	a.m.	
7:00	a.m.	
8:00	a.m.	
9:00	a.m.	
10:00	a.m.	
11:00	a.m.	
12:00	p.m.	
1:00	p.m.	
2:00	p.m.	
3:00	p.m.	
4:00	p.m.	
5:00	p.m.	
6:00	p.m.	
7:00	p.m.	
8:00	p.m.	
9:00	p.m.	
10:00	p.m.	
11:00	p.m.	
12:00	a.m.	

Daily Plan for Sunday, August 9, 2015

12:00	a.m.	
1:00	a.m.	
2:00	a.m.	
3:00	a.m.	
4:00	a.m.	
5:00	a.m.	
6:00	a.m.	
7:00	a.m.	
8:00	a.m.	
9:00	a.m.	
10:00	a.m.	
11:00	a.m.	
12:00	p.m.	
1:00	p.m.	
2:00	p.m.	
3:00	p.m.	
4:00	p.m.	
5:00	p.m.	
6:00	p.m.	
7:00	p.m.	
8:00	p.m.	
9:00	p.m.	
10:00	p.m.	
11:00	p.m.	
12:00	a.m.	

Daily Plan for Monday, August 10, 2015

12:00	a.m.	
1:00	a.m.	
2:00	a.m.	
3:00	a.m.	
4:00	a.m.	
5:00	a.m.	
6:00	a.m.	
7:00	a.m.	
8:00	a.m.	
9:00	a.m.	
10:00	a.m.	
11:00	a.m.	
12:00	p.m.	
1:00	p.m.	
2:00	p.m.	
3:00	p.m.	
4:00	p.m.	
5:00	p.m.	
6:00	p.m.	
7:00	p.m.	
8:00	p.m.	
9:00	p.m.	
10:00	p.m.	
11:00	p.m.	
12:00	a.m.	

Daily Plan for Tuesday, August 11, 2015

12:00	a.m.	
1:00	a.m.	
2:00	a.m.	
3:00	a.m.	
4:00	a.m.	
5:00	a.m.	
6:00	a.m.	
7:00	a.m.	
8:00	a.m.	
9:00	a.m.	
10:00	a.m.	
11:00	a.m.	
12:00	p.m.	
1:00	p.m.	
2:00	p.m.	
3:00	p.m.	
4:00	p.m.	
5:00	p.m.	
6:00	p.m.	
7:00	p.m.	
8:00	p.m.	
9:00	p.m.	
10:00	p.m.	
11:00	p.m.	
12:00	a.m.	

Daily Plan for Wednesday, August 12, 2015

Time		
12:00	a.m.	
1:00	a.m.	
2:00	a.m.	
3:00	a.m.	
4:00	a.m.	
5:00	a.m.	
6:00	a.m.	
7:00	a.m.	
8:00	a.m.	
9:00	a.m.	
10:00	a.m.	
11:00	a.m.	
12:00	p.m.	
1:00	p.m.	
2:00	p.m.	
3:00	p.m.	
4:00	p.m.	
5:00	p.m.	
6:00	p.m.	
7:00	p.m.	
8:00	p.m.	
9:00	p.m.	
10:00	p.m.	
11:00	p.m.	
12:00	a.m.	

Daily Plan for Thursday, August 13, 2015

12:00	a.m.	
1:00	a.m.	
2:00	a.m.	
3:00	a.m.	
4:00	a.m.	
5:00	a.m.	
6:00	a.m.	
7:00	a.m.	
8:00	a.m.	
9:00	a.m.	
10:00	a.m.	
11:00	a.m.	
12:00	p.m.	
1:00	p.m.	
2:00	p.m.	
3:00	p.m.	
4:00	p.m.	
5:00	p.m.	
6:00	p.m.	
7:00	p.m.	
8:00	p.m.	
9:00	p.m.	
10:00	p.m.	
11:00	p.m.	
12:00	a.m.	

Daily Plan for Friday, August 14, 2015

12:00	a.m.	
1:00	a.m.	
2:00	a.m.	
3:00	a.m.	
4:00	a.m.	
5:00	a.m.	
6:00	a.m.	
7:00	a.m.	
8:00	a.m.	
9:00	a.m.	
10:00	a.m.	
11:00	a.m.	
12:00	p.m.	
1:00	p.m.	
2:00	p.m.	
3:00	p.m.	
4:00	p.m.	
5:00	p.m.	
6:00	p.m.	
7:00	p.m.	
8:00	p.m.	
9:00	p.m.	
10:00	p.m.	
11:00	p.m.	
12:00	a.m.	

Daily Plan for Saturday, August 15, 2015

12:00	a.m.	
1:00	a.m.	
2:00	a.m.	
3:00	a.m.	
4:00	a.m.	
5:00	a.m.	
6:00	a.m.	
7:00	a.m.	
8:00	a.m.	
9:00	a.m.	
10:00	a.m.	
11:00	a.m.	
12:00	p.m.	
1:00	p.m.	
2:00	p.m.	
3:00	p.m.	
4:00	p.m.	
5:00	p.m.	
6:00	p.m.	
7:00	p.m.	
8:00	p.m.	
9:00	p.m.	
10:00	p.m.	
11:00	p.m.	
12:00	a.m.	

Daily Plan for Sunday, August 16, 2015

12:00	a.m.	
1:00	a.m.	
2:00	a.m.	
3:00	a.m.	
p4:00	a.m.	
5:00	a.m.	
6:00	a.m.	
7:00	a.m.	
8:00	a.m.	
9:00	a.m.	
10:00	a.m.	
11:00	a.m.	
12:00	p.m.	
1:00	p.m.	
2:00	p.m.	
3:00	p.m.	
4:00	p.m.	
5:00	p.m.	
6:00	p.m.	
7:00	p.m.	
8:00	p.m.	
9:00	p.m.	
10:00	p.m.	
11:00	p.m.	
12:00	a.m.	

Daily Plan for Monday, August 17, 2015

12:00	a.m.	
1:00	a.m.	
2:00	a.m.	
3:00	a.m.	
4:00	a.m.	
5:00	a.m.	
6:00	a.m.	
7:00	a.m.	
8:00	a.m.	
9:00	a.m.	
10:00	a.m.	
11:00	a.m.	
12:00	p.m.	
1:00	p.m.	
2:00	p.m.	
3:00	p.m.	
4:00	p.m.	
5:00	p.m.	
6:00	p.m.	
7:00	p.m.	
8:00	p.m.	
9:00	p.m.	
10:00	p.m.	
11:00	p.m.	
12:00	a.m.	

Daily Plan for Tuesday, August 18, 2015

Time		
12:00	a.m.	
1:00	a.m.	
2:00	a.m.	
3:00	a.m.	
4:00	a.m.	
5:00	a.m.	
6:00	a.m.	
7:00	a.m.	
8:00	a.m.	
9:00	a.m.	
10:00	a.m.	
11:00	a.m.	
12:00	p.m.	
1:00	p.m.	
2:00	p.m.	
3:00	p.m.	
4:00	p.m.	
5:00	p.m.	
6:00	p.m.	
7:00	p.m.	
8:00	p.m.	
9:00	p.m.	
10:00	p.m.	
11:00	p.m.	
12:00	a.m.	

Daily Plan for Wednesday, August 19, 2015

12:00	a.m.	
1:00	a.m.	
2:00	a.m.	
3:00	a.m.	
4:00	a.m.	
5:00	a.m.	
6:00	a.m.	
7:00	a.m.	
8:00	a.m.	
9:00	a.m.	
10:00	a.m.	
11:00	a.m.	
12:00	p.m.	
1:00	p.m.	
2:00	p.m.	
3:00	p.m.	
4:00	p.m.	
5:00	p.m.	
6:00	p.m.	
7:00	p.m.	
8:00	p.m.	
9:00	p.m.	
10:00	p.m.	
11:00	p.m.	
12:00	a.m.	

Daily Plan for Thursday, August 20, 2015

12:00	a.m.	
1:00	a.m.	
2:00	a.m.	
3:00	a.m.	
4:00	a.m.	
5:00	a.m.	
6:00	a.m.	
7:00	a.m.	
8:00	a.m.	
9:00	a.m.	
10:00	a.m.	
11:00	a.m.	
12:00	p.m.	
1:00	p.m.	
2:00	p.m.	
3:00	p.m.	
4:00	p.m.	
5:00	p.m.	
6:00	p.m.	
7:00	p.m.	
8:00	p.m.	
9:00	p.m.	
10:00	p.m.	
11:00	p.m.	
12:00	a.m.	

Daily Plan for Friday, August 21, 2015

12:00	a.m.	
1:00	a.m.	
2:00	a.m.	
3:00	a.m.	
4:00	a.m.	
5:00	a.m.	
6:00	a.m.	
7:00	a.m.	
8:00	a.m.	
9:00	a.m.	
10:00	a.m.	
11:00	a.m.	
12:00	p.m.	
1:00	p.m.	
2:00	p.m.	
3:00	p.m.	
4:00	p.m.	
5:00	p.m.	
6:00	p.m.	
7:00	p.m.	
8:00	p.m.	
9:00	p.m.	
10:00	p.m.	
11:00	p.m.	
12:00	a.m.	

Daily Plan for Saturday, August 22, 2015

Time		
12:00	a.m.	
1:00	a.m.	
2:00	a.m.	
3:00	a.m.	
4:00	a.m.	
5:00	a.m.	
6:00	a.m.	
7:00	a.m.	
8:00	a.m.	
9:00	a.m.	
10:00	a.m.	
11:00	a.m.	
12:00	p.m.	
1:00	p.m.	
2:00	p.m.	
3:00	p.m.	
4:00	p.m.	
5:00	p.m.	
6:00	p.m.	
7:00	p.m.	
8:00	p.m.	
9:00	p.m.	
10:00	p.m.	
11:00	p.m.	
12:00	a.m.	

Daily Plan for Sunday, August 23, 2015

Time	
12:00 a.m.	
1:00 a.m.	
2:00 a.m.	
3:00 a.m.	
4:00 a.m.	
5:00 a.m.	
6:00 a.m.	
7:00 a.m.	
8:00 a.m.	
9:00 a.m.	
10:00 a.m.	
11:00 a.m.	
12:00 p.m.	
1:00 p.m.	
2:00 p.m.	
3:00 p.m.	
4:00 p.m.	
5:00 p.m.	
6:00 p.m.	
7:00 p.m.	
8:00 p.m.	
9:00 p.m.	
10:00 p.m.	
11:00 p.m.	
12:00 a.m.	

Daily Plan for Monday, August 24, 2015

12:00	a.m.	
1:00	a.m.	
2:00	a.m.	
3:00	a.m.	
4:00	a.m.	
5:00	a.m.	
6:00	a.m.	
7:00	a.m.	
8:00	a.m.	
9:00	a.m.	
10:00	a.m.	
11:00	a.m.	
12:00	p.m.	
1:00	p.m.	
2:00	p.m.	
3:00	p.m.	
4:00	p.m.	
5:00	p.m.	
6:00	p.m.	
7:00	p.m.	
8:00	p.m.	
9:00	p.m.	
10:00	p.m.	
11:00	p.m.	
12:00	a.m.	

Daily Plan for Tuesday, August 25, 2015

12:00	a.m.	
1:00	a.m.	
2:00	a.m.	
3:00	a.m.	
4:00	a.m.	
5:00	a.m.	
6:00	a.m.	
7:00	a.m.	
8:00	a.m.	
9:00	a.m.	
10:00	a.m.	
11:00	a.m.	
12:00	p.m.	
1:00	p.m.	
2:00	p.m.	
3:00	p.m.	
4:00	p.m.	
5:00	p.m.	
6:00	p.m.	
7:00	p.m.	
8:00	p.m.	
9:00	p.m.	
10:00	p.m.	
11:00	p.m.	
12:00	a.m.	

Daily Plan for Wednesday, August 26, 2015

12:00 a.m.	
1:00 a.m.	
2:00 a.m.	
3:00 a.m.	
4:00 a.m.	
5:00 a.m.	
6:00 a.m.	
7:00 a.m.	
8:00 a.m.	
9:00 a.m.	
10:00 a.m.	
11:00 a.m.	
12:00 p.m.	
1:00 p.m.	
2:00 p.m.	
3:00 p.m.	
4:00 p.m.	
5:00 p.m.	
6:00 p.m.	
7:00 p.m.	
8:00 p.m.	
9:00 p.m.	
10:00 p.m.	
11:00 p.m.	
12:00 a.m.	

Daily Plan for Thursday, August 27, 2015

12:00	a.m.	
1:00	a.m.	
2:00	a.m.	
3:00	a.m.	
4:00	a.m.	
5:00	a.m.	
6:00	a.m.	
7:00	a.m.	
8:00	a.m.	
9:00	a.m.	
10:00	a.m.	
11:00	a.m.	
12:00	p.m.	
1:00	p.m.	
2:00	p.m.	
3:00	p.m.	
4:00	p.m.	
5:00	p.m.	
6:00	p.m.	
7:00	p.m.	
8:00	p.m.	
9:00	p.m.	
10:00	p.m.	
11:00	p.m.	
12:00	a.m.	

Daily Plan for Friday, August 28, 2015

12:00	a.m.	
1:00	a.m.	
2:00	a.m.	
3:00	a.m.	
4:00	a.m.	
5:00	a.m.	
6:00	a.m.	
7:00	a.m.	
8:00	a.m.	
9:00	a.m.	
10:00	a.m.	
11:00	a.m.	
12:00	p.m.	
1:00	p.m.	
2:00	p.m.	
3:00	p.m.	
4:00	p.m.	
5:00	p.m.	
6:00	p.m.	
7:00	p.m.	
8:00	p.m.	
9:00	p.m.	
10:00	p.m.	
11:00	p.m.	
12:00	a.m.	

Daily Plan for Saturday, August 29, 2015

Time	
12:00 a.m.	
1:00 a.m.	
2:00 a.m.	
3:00 a.m.	
4:00 a.m.	
5:00 a.m.	
6:00 a.m.	
7:00 a.m.	
8:00 a.m.	
9:00 a.m.	
10:00 a.m.	
11:00 a.m.	
12:00 p.m.	
1:00 p.m.	
2:00 p.m.	
3:00 p.m.	
4:00 p.m.	
5:00 p.m.	
6:00 p.m.	
7:00 p.m.	
8:00 p.m.	
9:00 p.m.	
10:00 p.m.	
11:00 p.m.	
12:00 a.m.	

Daily Plan for Sunday, August 30, 2015

Time		
12:00	a.m.	
1:00	a.m.	
2:00	a.m.	
3:00	a.m.	
4:00	a.m.	
5:00	a.m.	
6:00	a.m.	
7:00	a.m.	
8:00	a.m.	
9:00	a.m.	
10:00	a.m.	
11:00	a.m.	
12:00	p.m.	
1:00	p.m.	
2:00	p.m.	
3:00	p.m.	
4:00	p.m.	
5:00	p.m.	
6:00	p.m.	
7:00	p.m.	
8:00	p.m.	
9:00	p.m.	
10:00	p.m.	
11:00	p.m.	
12:00	a.m.	

Daily Plan for Monday, August 31, 2015

12:00	a.m.	
1:00	a.m.	
2:00	a.m.	
3:00	a.m.	
4:00	a.m.	
5:00	a.m.	
6:00	a.m.	
7:00	a.m.	
8:00	a.m.	
9:00	a.m.	
10:00	a.m.	
11:00	a.m.	
12:00	p.m.	
1:00	p.m.	
2:00	p.m.	
3:00	p.m.	
4:00	p.m.	
5:00	p.m.	
6:00	p.m.	
7:00	p.m.	
8:00	p.m.	
9:00	p.m.	
10:00	p.m.	
11:00	p.m.	
12:00	a.m.	

Daily Plan for Tuesday, September 1, 2015

Time		
12:00	a.m.	
1:00	a.m.	
2:00	a.m.	
3:00	a.m.	
4:00	a.m.	
5:00	a.m.	
6:00	a.m.	
7:00	a.m.	
8:00	a.m.	
9:00	a.m.	
10:00	a.m.	
11:00	a.m.	
12:00	p.m.	
1:00	p.m.	
2:00	p.m.	
3:00	p.m.	
4:00	p.m.	
5:00	p.m.	
6:00	p.m.	
7:00	p.m.	
8:00	p.m.	
9:00	p.m.	
10:00	p.m.	
11:00	p.m.	
12:00	a.m.	

Daily Plan for Wednesday, September 2, 2015

12:00	a.m.	
1:00	a.m.	
2:00	a.m.	
3:00	a.m.	
4:00	a.m.	
5:00	a.m.	
6:00	a.m.	
7:00	a.m.	
8:00	a.m.	
9:00	a.m.	
10:00	a.m.	
11:00	a.m.	
12:00	p.m.	
1:00	p.m.	
2:00	p.m.	
3:00	p.m.	
4:00	p.m.	
5:00	p.m.	
6:00	p.m.	
7:00	p.m.	
8:00	p.m.	
9:00	p.m.	
10:00	p.m.	
11:00	p.m.	
12:00	a.m.	

Daily Plan for Thursday, September 3, 2015

12:00	a.m.	
1:00	a.m.	
2:00	a.m.	
3:00	a.m.	
4:00	a.m.	
5:00	a.m.	
6:00	a.m.	
7:00	a.m.	
8:00	a.m.	
9:00	a.m.	
10:00	a.m.	
11:00	a.m.	
12:00	p.m.	
1:00	p.m.	
2:00	p.m.	
3:00	p.m.	
4:00	p.m.	
5:00	p.m.	
6:00	p.m.	
7:00	p.m.	
8:00	p.m.	
9:00	p.m.	
10:00	p.m.	
11:00	p.m.	
12:00	a.m.	

Daily Plan for Friday, September 4, 2015

12:00	a.m.	
1:00	a.m.	
2:00	a.m.	
3:00	a.m.	
4:00	a.m.	
5:00	a.m.	
6:00	a.m.	
7:00	a.m.	
8:00	a.m.	
9:00	a.m.	
10:00	a.m.	
11:00	a.m.	
12:00	p.m.	
1:00	p.m.	
2:00	p.m.	
3:00	p.m.	
4:00	p.m.	
5:00	p.m.	
6:00	p.m.	
7:00	p.m.	
8:00	p.m.	
9:00	p.m.	
10:00	p.m.	
11:00	p.m.	
12:00	a.m.	

Daily Plan for Saturday, September 5, 2015

Time		
12:00	a.m.	
1:00	a.m.	
2:00	a.m.	
3:00	a.m.	
4:00	a.m.	
5:00	a.m.	
6:00	a.m.	
7:00	a.m.	
8:00	a.m.	
9:00	a.m.	
10:00	a.m.	
11:00	a.m.	
12:00	p.m.	
1:00	p.m.	
2:00	p.m.	
3:00	p.m.	
4:00	p.m.	
5:00	p.m.	
6:00	p.m.	
7:00	p.m.	
8:00	p.m.	
9:00	p.m.	
10:00	p.m.	
11:00	p.m.	
12:00	a.m.	

Daily Plan for Sunday, September 6, 2015

12:00	a.m.	
1:00	a.m.	
2:00	a.m.	
3:00	a.m.	
4:00	a.m.	
5:00	a.m.	
6:00	a.m.	
7:00	a.m.	
8:00	a.m.	
9:00	a.m.	
10:00	a.m.	
11:00	a.m.	
12:00	p.m.	
1:00	p.m.	
2:00	p.m.	
3:00	p.m.	
4:00	p.m.	
5:00	p.m.	
6:00	p.m.	
7:00	p.m.	
8:00	p.m.	
9:00	p.m.	
10:00	p.m.	
11:00	p.m.	
12:00	a.m.	

Daily Plan for Monday, September 7, 2015

Time		
12:00	a.m.	
1:00	a.m.	
2:00	a.m.	
3:00	a.m.	
4:00	a.m.	
5:00	a.m.	
6:00	a.m.	
7:00	a.m.	
8:00	a.m.	
9:00	a.m.	
10:00	a.m.	
11:00	a.m.	
12:00	p.m.	
1:00	p.m.	
2:00	p.m.	
3:00	p.m.	
4:00	p.m.	
5:00	p.m.	
6:00	p.m.	
7:00	p.m.	
8:00	p.m.	
9:00	p.m.	
10:00	p.m.	
11:00	p.m.	
12:00	a.m.	

Daily Plan for Tuesday, September 8, 2015

12:00	a.m.	
1:00	a.m.	
2:00	a.m.	
3:00	a.m.	
4:00	a.m.	
5:00	a.m.	
6:00	a.m.	
7:00	a.m.	
8:00	a.m.	
9:00	a.m.	
10:00	a.m.	
11:00	a.m.	
12:00	p.m.	
1:00	p.m.	
2:00	p.m.	
3:00	p.m.	
4:00	p.m.	
5:00	p.m.	
6:00	p.m.	
7:00	p.m.	
8:00	p.m.	
9:00	p.m.	
10:00	p.m.	
11:00	p.m.	
12:00	a.m.	

Daily Plan for Wednesday, September 9, 2015

12:00	a.m.	
1:00	a.m.	
2:00	a.m.	
3:00	a.m.	
4:00	a.m.	
5:00	a.m.	
6:00	a.m.	
7:00	a.m.	
8:00	a.m.	
9:00	a.m.	
10:00	a.m.	
11:00	a.m.	
12:00	p.m.	
1:00	p.m.	
2:00	p.m.	
3:00	p.m.	
4:00	p.m.	
5:00	p.m.	
6:00	p.m.	
7:00	p.m.	
8:00	p.m.	
9:00	p.m.	
10:00	p.m.	
11:00	p.m.	
12:00	a.m.	

Daily Plan for Thursday, September 10, 2015

12:00	a.m.	
1:00	a.m.	
2:00	a.m.	
3:00	a.m.	
4:00	a.m.	
5:00	a.m.	
6:00	a.m.	
7:00	a.m.	
8:00	a.m.	
9:00	a.m.	
10:00	a.m.	
11:00	a.m.	
12:00	p.m.	
1:00	p.m.	
2:00	p.m.	
3:00	p.m.	
4:00	p.m.	
5:00	p.m.	
6:00	p.m.	
7:00	p.m.	
8:00	p.m.	
9:00	p.m.	
10:00	p.m.	
11:00	p.m.	
12:00	a.m.	

Daily Plan for Friday, September 11, 2015

12:00	a.m.	
1:00	a.m.	
2:00	a.m.	
3:00	a.m.	
4:00	a.m.	
5:00	a.m.	
6:00	a.m.	
7:00	a.m.	
8:00	a.m.	
9:00	a.m.	
10:00	a.m.	
11:00	a.m.	
12:00	p.m.	
1:00	p.m.	
2:00	p.m.	
3:00	p.m.	
4:00	p.m.	
5:00	p.m.	
6:00	p.m.	
7:00	p.m.	
8:00	p.m.	
9:00	p.m.	
10:00	p.m.	
11:00	p.m.	
12:00	a.m.	

Daily Plan for Saturday, September 12, 2015

12:00	a.m.	
1:00	a.m.	
2:00	a.m.	
3:00	a.m.	
4:00	a.m.	
5:00	a.m.	
6:00	a.m.	
7:00	a.m.	
8:00	a.m.	
9:00	a.m.	
10:00	a.m.	
11:00	a.m.	
12:00	p.m.	
1:00	p.m.	
2:00	p.m.	
3:00	p.m.	
4:00	p.m.	
5:00	p.m.	
6:00	p.m.	
7:00	p.m.	
8:00	p.m.	
9:00	p.m.	
10:00	p.m.	
11:00	p.m.	
12:00	a.m.	

Daily Plan for Sunday, September 13, 2015

12:00	a.m.	
1:00	a.m.	
2:00	a.m.	
3:00	a.m.	
4:00	a.m.	
5:00	a.m.	
6:00	a.m.	
7:00	a.m.	
8:00	a.m.	
9:00	a.m.	
10:00	a.m.	
11:00	a.m.	
12:00	p.m.	
1:00	p.m.	
2:00	p.m.	
3:00	p.m.	
4:00	p.m.	
5:00	p.m.	
6:00	p.m.	
7:00	p.m.	
8:00	p.m.	
9:00	p.m.	
10:00	p.m.	
11:00	p.m.	
12:00	a.m.	

Daily Plan for Monday, September 14, 2015

12:00	a.m.	
1:00	a.m.	
2:00	a.m.	
3:00	a.m.	
4:00	a.m.	
5:00	a.m.	
6:00	a.m.	
7:00	a.m.	
8:00	a.m.	
9:00	a.m.	
10:00	a.m.	
11:00	a.m.	
12:00	p.m.	
1:00	p.m.	
2:00	p.m.	
3:00	p.m.	
4:00	p.m.	
5:00	p.m.	
6:00	p.m.	
7:00	p.m.	
8:00	p.m.	
9:00	p.m.	
10:00	p.m.	
11:00	p.m.	
12:00	a.m.	

Daily Plan for Tuesday, September 15, 2015

12:00	a.m.	
1:00	a.m.	
2:00	a.m.	
3:00	a.m.	
4:00	a.m.	
5:00	a.m.	
6:00	a.m.	
7:00	a.m.	
8:00	a.m.	
9:00	a.m.	
10:00	a.m.	
11:00	a.m.	
12:00	p.m.	
1:00	p.m.	
2:00	p.m.	
3:00	p.m.	
4:00	p.m.	
5:00	p.m.	
6:00	p.m.	
7:00	p.m.	
8:00	p.m.	
9:00	p.m.	
10:00	p.m.	
11:00	p.m.	
12:00	a.m.	

Daily Plan for Wednesday, September 16, 2015

12:00	a.m.	
1:00	a.m.	
2:00	a.m.	
3:00	a.m.	
4:00	a.m.	
5:00	a.m.	
6:00	a.m.	
7:00	a.m.	
8:00	a.m.	
9:00	a.m.	
10:00	a.m.	
11:00	a.m.	
12:00	p.m.	
1:00	p.m.	
2:00	p.m.	
3:00	p.m.	
4:00	p.m.	
5:00	p.m.	
6:00	p.m.	
7:00	p.m.	
8:00	p.m.	
9:00	p.m.	
10:00	p.m.	
11:00	p.m.	
12:00	a.m.	

Daily Plan for Thursday, September 17, 2015

12:00	a.m.	
1:00	a.m.	
2:00	a.m.	
3:00	a.m.	
4:00	a.m.	
5:00	a.m.	
6:00	a.m.	
7:00	a.m.	
8:00	a.m.	
9:00	a.m.	
10:00	a.m.	
11:00	a.m.	
12:00	p.m.	
1:00	p.m.	
2:00	p.m.	
3:00	p.m.	
4:00	p.m.	
5:00	p.m.	
6:00	p.m.	
7:00	p.m.	
8:00	p.m.	
9:00	p.m.	
10:00	p.m.	
11:00	p.m.	
12:00	a.m.	

Daily Plan for Friday, September 18, 2015

12:00	a.m.	
1:00	a.m.	
2:00	a.m.	
3:00	a.m.	
4:00	a.m.	
5:00	a.m.	
6:00	a.m.	
7:00	a.m.	
8:00	a.m.	
9:00	a.m.	
10:00	a.m.	
11:00	a.m.	
12:00	p.m.	
1:00	p.m.	
2:00	p.m.	
3:00	p.m.	
4:00	p.m.	
5:00	p.m.	
6:00	p.m.	
7:00	p.m.	
8:00	p.m.	
9:00	p.m.	
10:00	p.m.	
11:00	p.m.	
12:00	a.m.	

Daily Plan for Saturday, September 19, 2015

12:00	a.m.	
1:00	a.m.	
2:00	a.m.	
3:00	a.m.	
4:00	a.m.	
5:00	a.m.	
6:00	a.m.	
7:00	a.m.	
8:00	a.m.	
9:00	a.m.	
10:00	a.m.	
11:00	a.m.	
12:00	p.m.	
1:00	p.m.	
2:00	p.m.	
3:00	p.m.	
4:00	p.m.	
5:00	p.m.	
6:00	p.m.	
7:00	p.m.	
8:00	p.m.	
9:00	p.m.	
10:00	p.m.	
11:00	p.m.	
12:00	a.m.	

Daily Plan for Sunday, September 20, 2015

12:00	a.m.	
1:00	a.m.	
2:00	a.m.	
3:00	a.m.	
4:00	a.m.	
5:00	a.m.	
6:00	a.m.	
7:00	a.m.	
8:00	a.m.	
9:00	a.m.	
10:00	a.m.	
11:00	a.m.	
12:00	p.m.	
1:00	p.m.	
2:00	p.m.	
3:00	p.m.	
4:00	p.m.	
5:00	p.m.	
6:00	p.m.	
7:00	p.m.	
8:00	p.m.	
9:00	p.m.	
10:00	p.m.	
11:00	p.m.	
12:00	a.m.	

Daily Plan for Monday, September 21, 2015

12:00	a.m.	
1:00	a.m.	
2:00	a.m.	
3:00	a.m.	
4:00	a.m.	
5:00	a.m.	
6:00	a.m.	
7:00	a.m.	
8:00	a.m.	
9:00	a.m.	
10:00	a.m.	
11:00	a.m.	
12:00	p.m.	
1:00	p.m.	
2:00	p.m.	
3:00	p.m.	
4:00	p.m.	
5:00	p.m.	
6:00	p.m.	
7:00	p.m.	
8:00	p.m.	
9:00	p.m.	
10:00	p.m.	
11:00	p.m.	
12:00	a.m.	

Daily Plan for Tuesday, September 22, 2015

12:00	a.m.	
1:00	a.m.	
2:00	a.m.	
3:00	a.m.	
4:00	a.m.	
5:00	a.m.	
6:00	a.m.	
7:00	a.m.	
8:00	a.m.	
9:00	a.m.	
10:00	a.m.	
11:00	a.m.	
12:00	p.m.	
1:00	p.m.	
2:00	p.m.	
3:00	p.m.	
4:00	p.m.	
5:00	p.m.	
6:00	p.m.	
7:00	p.m.	
8:00	p.m.	
9:00	p.m.	
10:00	p.m.	
11:00	p.m.	
12:00	a.m.	

Daily Plan for Wednesday, September 23, 2015

12:00	a.m.	
1:00	a.m.	
2:00	a.m.	
3:00	a.m.	
4:00	a.m.	
5:00	a.m.	
6:00	a.m.	
7:00	a.m.	
8:00	a.m.	
9:00	a.m.	
10:00	a.m.	
11:00	a.m.	
12:00	p.m.	
1:00	p.m.	
2:00	p.m.	
3:00	p.m.	
4:00	p.m.	
5:00	p.m.	
6:00	p.m.	
7:00	p.m.	
8:00	p.m.	
9:00	p.m.	
10:00	p.m.	
11:00	p.m.	
12:00	a.m.	

Daily Plan for Thursday, September 24, 2015

12:00	a.m.	
1:00	a.m.	
2:00	a.m.	
3:00	a.m.	
4:00	a.m.	
5:00	a.m.	
6:00	a.m.	
7:00	a.m.	
8:00	a.m.	
9:00	a.m.	
10:00	a.m.	
11:00	a.m.	
12:00	p.m.	
1:00	p.m.	
2:00	p.m.	
3:00	p.m.	
4:00	p.m.	
5:00	p.m.	
6:00	p.m.	
7:00	p.m.	
8:00	p.m.	
9:00	p.m.	
10:00	p.m.	
11:00	p.m.	
12:00	a.m.	

Daily Plan for Friday, September 25, 2015

Time	
12:00 a.m.	
1:00 a.m.	
2:00 a.m.	
3:00 a.m.	
4:00 a.m.	
5:00 a.m.	
6:00 a.m.	
7:00 a.m.	
8:00 a.m.	
9:00 a.m.	
10:00 a.m.	
11:00 a.m.	
12:00 p.m.	
1:00 p.m.	
2:00 p.m.	
3:00 p.m.	
4:00 p.m.	
5:00 p.m.	
6:00 p.m.	
7:00 p.m.	
8:00 p.m.	
9:00 p.m.	
10:00 p.m.	
11:00 p.m.	
12:00 a.m.	

Daily Plan for Saturday, September 26, 2015

12:00	a.m.	
1:00	a.m.	
2:00	a.m.	
3:00	a.m.	
4:00	a.m.	
5:00	a.m.	
6:00	a.m.	
7:00	a.m.	
8:00	a.m.	
9:00	a.m.	
10:00	a.m.	
11:00	a.m.	
12:00	p.m.	
1:00	p.m.	
2:00	p.m.	
3:00	p.m.	
4:00	p.m.	
5:00	p.m.	
6:00	p.m.	
7:00	p.m.	
8:00	p.m.	
9:00	p.m.	
10:00	p.m.	
11:00	p.m.	
12:00	a.m.	

Daily Plan for Sunday, September 27, 2015

Time	
12:00 a.m.	
1:00 a.m.	
2:00 a.m.	
3:00 a.m.	
4:00 a.m.	
5:00 a.m.	
6:00 a.m.	
7:00 a.m.	
8:00 a.m.	
9:00 a.m.	
10:00 a.m.	
11:00 a.m.	
12:00 p.m.	
1:00 p.m.	
2:00 p.m.	
3:00 p.m.	
4:00 p.m.	
5:00 p.m.	
6:00 p.m.	
7:00 p.m.	
8:00 p.m.	
9:00 p.m.	
10:00 p.m.	
11:00 p.m.	
12:00 a.m.	

Daily Plan for Monday, September 28, 2015

12:00	a.m.	
1:00	a.m.	
2:00	a.m.	
3:00	a.m.	
4:00	a.m.	
5:00	a.m.	
6:00	a.m.	
7:00	a.m.	
8:00	a.m.	
9:00	a.m.	
10:00	a.m.	
11:00	a.m.	
12:00	p.m.	
1:00	p.m.	
2:00	p.m.	
3:00	p.m.	
4:00	p.m.	
5:00	p.m.	
6:00	p.m.	
7:00	p.m.	
8:00	p.m.	
9:00	p.m.	
10:00	p.m.	
11:00	p.m.	
12:00	a.m.	

Daily Plan for Tuesday, September 29, 2015

12:00	a.m.	
1:00	a.m.	
2:00	a.m.	
3:00	a.m.	
4:00	a.m.	
5:00	a.m.	
6:00	a.m.	
7:00	a.m.	
8:00	a.m.	
9:00	a.m.	
10:00	a.m.	
11:00	a.m.	
12:00	p.m.	
1:00	p.m.	
2:00	p.m.	
3:00	p.m.	
4:00	p.m.	
5:00	p.m.	
6:00	p.m.	
7:00	p.m.	
8:00	p.m.	
9:00	p.m.	
10:00	p.m.	
11:00	p.m.	
12:00	a.m.	

Daily Plan for Wednesday, September 30, 2015

12:00	a.m.	
1:00	a.m.	
2:00	a.m.	
3:00	a.m.	
4:00	a.m.	
5:00	a.m.	
6:00	a.m.	
7:00	a.m.	
8:00	a.m.	
9:00	a.m.	
10:00	a.m.	
11:00	a.m.	
12:00	p.m.	
1:00	p.m.	
2:00	p.m.	
3:00	p.m.	
4:00	p.m.	
5:00	p.m.	
6:00	p.m.	
7:00	p.m.	
8:00	p.m.	
9:00	p.m.	
10:00	p.m.	
11:00	p.m.	
12:00	a.m.	

Daily Plan for Thursday, October 1, 2015

12:00	a.m.	
1:00	a.m.	
2:00	a.m.	
3:00	a.m.	
4:00	a.m.	
5:00	a.m.	
6:00	a.m.	
7:00	a.m.	
8:00	a.m.	
9:00	a.m.	
10:00	a.m.	
11:00	a.m.	
12:00	p.m.	
1:00	p.m.	
2:00	p.m.	
3:00	p.m.	
4:00	p.m.	
5:00	p.m.	
6:00	p.m.	
7:00	p.m.	
8:00	p.m.	
9:00	p.m.	
10:00	p.m.	
11:00	p.m.	
12:00	a.m.	

Daily Plan for Friday, October 2, 2015

12:00	a.m.	
1:00	a.m.	
2:00	a.m.	
3:00	a.m.	
4:00	a.m.	
5:00	a.m.	
6:00	a.m.	
7:00	a.m.	
8:00	a.m.	
9:00	a.m.	
10:00	a.m.	
11:00	a.m.	
12:00	p.m.	
1:00	p.m.	
2:00	p.m.	
3:00	p.m.	
4:00	p.m.	
5:00	p.m.	
6:00	p.m.	
7:00	p.m.	
8:00	p.m.	
9:00	p.m.	
10:00	p.m.	
11:00	p.m.	
12:00	a.m.	

Daily Plan for Saturday, October 3, 2015

12:00	a.m.	
1:00	a.m.	
2:00	a.m.	
3:00	a.m.	
4:00	a.m.	
5:00	a.m.	
6:00	a.m.	
7:00	a.m.	
8:00	a.m.	
9:00	a.m.	
10:00	a.m.	
11:00	a.m.	
12:00	p.m.	
1:00	p.m.	
2:00	p.m.	
3:00	p.m.	
4:00	p.m.	
5:00	p.m.	
6:00	p.m.	
7:00	p.m.	
8:00	p.m.	
9:00	p.m.	
10:00	p.m.	
11:00	p.m.	
12:00	a.m.	

Daily Plan for Sunday, October 4, 2015

12:00	a.m.	
1:00	a.m.	
2:00	a.m.	
3:00	a.m.	
4:00	a.m.	
5:00	a.m.	
6:00	a.m.	
7:00	a.m.	
8:00	a.m.	
9:00	a.m.	
10:00	a.m.	
11:00	a.m.	
12:00	p.m.	
1:00	p.m.	
2:00	p.m.	
3:00	p.m.	
4:00	p.m.	
5:00	p.m.	
6:00	p.m.	
7:00	p.m.	
8:00	p.m.	
9:00	p.m.	
10:00	p.m.	
11:00	p.m.	
12:00	a.m.	

Daily Plan for Monday, October 5, 2015

Time		
12:00	a.m.	
1:00	a.m.	
2:00	a.m.	
3:00	a.m.	
4:00	a.m.	
5:00	a.m.	
6:00	a.m.	
7:00	a.m.	
8:00	a.m.	
9:00	a.m.	
10:00	a.m.	
11:00	a.m.	
12:00	p.m.	
1:00	p.m.	
2:00	p.m.	
3:00	p.m.	
4:00	p.m.	
5:00	p.m.	
6:00	p.m.	
7:00	p.m.	
8:00	p.m.	
9:00	p.m.	
10:00	p.m.	
11:00	p.m.	
12:00	a.m.	

Daily Plan for Tuesday, October 6, 2015

12:00	a.m.	
1:00	a.m.	
2:00	a.m.	
3:00	a.m.	
4:00	a.m.	
5:00	a.m.	
6:00	a.m.	
7:00	a.m.	
8:00	a.m.	
9:00	a.m.	
10:00	a.m.	
11:00	a.m.	
12:00	p.m.	
1:00	p.m.	
2:00	p.m.	
3:00	p.m.	
4:00	p.m.	
5:00	p.m.	
6:00	p.m.	
7:00	p.m.	
8:00	p.m.	
9:00	p.m.	
10:00	p.m.	
11:00	p.m.	
12:00	a.m.	

Daily Plan for Wednesday, October 7, 2015

12:00	a.m.	
1:00	a.m.	
2:00	a.m.	
3:00	a.m.	
4:00	a.m.	
5:00	a.m.	
6:00	a.m.	
7:00	a.m.	
8:00	a.m.	
9:00	a.m.	
10:00	a.m.	
11:00	a.m.	
12:00	p.m.	
1:00	p.m.	
2:00	p.m.	
3:00	p.m.	
4:00	p.m.	
5:00	p.m.	
6:00	p.m.	
7:00	p.m.	
8:00	p.m.	
9:00	p.m.	
10:00	p.m.	
11:00	p.m.	
12:00	a.m.	

Daily Plan for Thursday, October 8, 2015

12:00	a.m.	
1:00	a.m.	
2:00	a.m.	
3:00	a.m.	
4:00	a.m.	
5:00	a.m.	
6:00	a.m.	
7:00	a.m.	
8:00	a.m.	
9:00	a.m.	
10:00	a.m.	
11:00	a.m.	
12:00	p.m.	
1:00	p.m.	
2:00	p.m.	
3:00	p.m.	
4:00	p.m.	
5:00	p.m.	
6:00	p.m.	
7:00	p.m.	
8:00	p.m.	
9:00	p.m.	
10:00	p.m.	
11:00	p.m.	
12:00	a.m.	

Daily Plan for Friday, October 9, 2015

12:00	a.m.	
1:00	a.m.	
2:00	a.m.	
3:00	a.m.	
4:00	a.m.	
5:00	a.m.	
6:00	a.m.	
7:00	a.m.	
8:00	a.m.	
9:00	a.m.	
10:00	a.m.	
11:00	a.m.	
12:00	p.m.	
1:00	p.m.	
2:00	p.m.	
3:00	p.m.	
4:00	p.m.	
5:00	p.m.	
6:00	p.m.	
7:00	p.m.	
8:00	p.m.	
9:00	p.m.	
10:00	p.m.	
11:00	p.m.	
12:00	a.m.	

Daily Plan for Saturday, October 10, 2015

Time	
12:00 a.m.	
1:00 a.m.	
2:00 a.m.	
3:00 a.m.	
4:00 a.m.	
5:00 a.m.	
6:00 a.m.	
7:00 a.m.	
8:00 a.m.	
9:00 a.m.	
10:00 a.m.	
11:00 a.m.	
12:00 p.m.	
1:00 p.m.	
2:00 p.m.	
3:00 p.m.	
4:00 p.m.	
5:00 p.m.	
6:00 p.m.	
7:00 p.m.	
8:00 p.m.	
9:00 p.m.	
10:00 p.m.	
11:00 p.m.	
12:00 a.m.	

Daily Plan for Sunday, October 11, 2015

12:00	a.m.	
1:00	a.m.	
2:00	a.m.	
3:00	a.m.	
4:00	a.m.	
5:00	a.m.	
6:00	a.m.	
7:00	a.m.	
8:00	a.m.	
9:00	a.m.	
10:00	a.m.	
11:00	a.m.	
12:00	p.m.	
1:00	p.m.	
2:00	p.m.	
3:00	p.m.	
4:00	p.m.	
5:00	p.m.	
6:00	p.m.	
7:00	p.m.	
8:00	p.m.	
9:00	p.m.	
10:00	p.m.	
11:00	p.m.	
12:00	a.m.	

Daily Plan for Monday, October 12, 2015

Time		
12:00	a.m.	
1:00	a.m.	
2:00	a.m.	
3:00	a.m.	
4:00	a.m.	
5:00	a.m.	
6:00	a.m.	
7:00	a.m.	
8:00	a.m.	
9:00	a.m.	
10:00	a.m.	
11:00	a.m.	
12:00	p.m.	
1:00	p.m.	
2:00	p.m.	
3:00	p.m.	
4:00	p.m.	
5:00	p.m.	
6:00	p.m.	
7:00	p.m.	
8:00	p.m.	
9:00	p.m.	
10:00	p.m.	
11:00	p.m.	
12:00	a.m.	

Daily Plan for Tuesday, October 13, 2015

12:00	a.m.	
1:00	a.m.	
2:00	a.m.	
3:00	a.m.	
4:00	a.m.	
5:00	a.m.	
6:00	a.m.	
7:00	a.m.	
8:00	a.m.	
9:00	a.m.	
10:00	a.m.	
11:00	a.m.	
12:00	p.m.	
1:00	p.m.	
2:00	p.m.	
3:00	p.m.	
4:00	p.m.	
5:00	p.m.	
6:00	p.m.	
7:00	p.m.	
8:00	p.m.	
9:00	p.m.	
10:00	p.m.	
11:00	p.m.	
12:00	a.m.	

Daily Plan for Wednesday, October 14, 2015

12:00	a.m.	
1:00	a.m.	
2:00	a.m.	
3:00	a.m.	
4:00	a.m.	
5:00	a.m.	
6:00	a.m.	
7:00	a.m.	
8:00	a.m.	
9:00	a.m.	
10:00	a.m.	
11:00	a.m.	
12:00	p.m.	
1:00	p.m.	
2:00	p.m.	
3:00	p.m.	
4:00	p.m.	
5:00	p.m.	
6:00	p.m.	
7:00	p.m.	
8:00	p.m.	
9:00	p.m.	
10:00	p.m.	
11:00	p.m.	
12:00	a.m.	

Daily Plan for Thursday, October 15, 2015

12:00	a.m.	
1:00	a.m.	
2:00	a.m.	
3:00	a.m.	
4:00	a.m.	
5:00	a.m.	
6:00	a.m.	
7:00	a.m.	
8:00	a.m.	
9:00	a.m.	
10:00	a.m.	
11:00	a.m.	
12:00	p.m.	
1:00	p.m.	
2:00	p.m.	
3:00	p.m.	
4:00	p.m.	
5:00	p.m.	
6:00	p.m.	
7:00	p.m.	
8:00	p.m.	
9:00	p.m.	
10:00	p.m.	
11:00	p.m.	
12:00	a.m.	

Daily Plan for Friday, October 16, 2015

12:00	a.m.	
1:00	a.m.	
2:00	a.m.	
3:00	a.m.	
4:00	a.m.	
5:00	a.m.	
6:00	a.m.	
7:00	a.m.	
8:00	a.m.	
9:00	a.m.	
10:00	a.m.	
11:00	a.m.	
12:00	p.m.	
1:00	p.m.	
2:00	p.m.	
3:00	p.m.	
4:00	p.m.	
5:00	p.m.	
6:00	p.m.	
7:00	p.m.	
8:00	p.m.	
9:00	p.m.	
10:00	p.m.	
11:00	p.m.	
12:00	a.m.	

Daily Plan for Saturday, October 17, 2015

12:00	a.m.	
1:00	a.m.	
2:00	a.m.	
3:00	a.m.	
4:00	a.m.	
5:00	a.m.	
6:00	a.m.	
7:00	a.m.	
8:00	a.m.	
9:00	a.m.	
10:00	a.m.	
11:00	a.m.	
12:00	p.m.	
1:00	p.m.	
2:00	p.m.	
3:00	p.m.	
4:00	p.m.	
5:00	p.m.	
6:00	p.m.	
7:00	p.m.	
8:00	p.m.	
9:00	p.m.	
10:00	p.m.	
11:00	p.m.	
12:00	a.m.	

Daily Plan for Sunday, October 18, 2015

Time		
12:00	a.m.	
1:00	a.m.	
2:00	a.m.	
3:00	a.m.	
4:00	a.m.	
5:00	a.m.	
6:00	a.m.	
7:00	a.m.	
8:00	a.m.	
9:00	a.m.	
10:00	a.m.	
11:00	a.m.	
12:00	p.m.	
1:00	p.m.	
2:00	p.m.	
3:00	p.m.	
4:00	p.m.	
5:00	p.m.	
6:00	p.m.	
7:00	p.m.	
8:00	p.m.	
9:00	p.m.	
10:00	p.m.	
11:00	p.m.	
12:00	a.m.	

Daily Plan for Monday, October 19, 2015

12:00	a.m.	
1:00	a.m.	
2:00	a.m.	
3:00	a.m.	
4:00	a.m.	
5:00	a.m.	
6:00	a.m.	
7:00	a.m.	
8:00	a.m.	
9:00	a.m.	
10:00	a.m.	
11:00	a.m.	
12:00	p.m.	
1:00	p.m.	
2:00	p.m.	
3:00	p.m.	
4:00	p.m.	
5:00	p.m.	
6:00	p.m.	
7:00	p.m.	
8:00	p.m.	
9:00	p.m.	
10:00	p.m.	
11:00	p.m.	
12:00	a.m.	

Daily Plan for Tuesday, October 20, 2015

12:00	a.m.	
1:00	a.m.	
2:00	a.m.	
3:00	a.m.	
4:00	a.m.	
5:00	a.m.	
6:00	a.m.	
7:00	a.m.	
8:00	a.m.	
9:00	a.m.	
10:00	a.m.	
11:00	a.m.	
12:00	p.m.	
1:00	p.m.	
2:00	p.m.	
3:00	p.m.	
4:00	p.m.	
5:00	p.m.	
6:00	p.m.	
7:00	p.m.	
8:00	p.m.	
9:00	p.m.	
10:00	p.m.	
11:00	p.m.	
12:00	a.m.	

Daily Plan for Wednesday, October 21, 2015

12:00	a.m.	
1:00	a.m.	
2:00	a.m.	
3:00	a.m.	
4:00	a.m.	
5:00	a.m.	
6:00	a.m.	
7:00	a.m.	
8:00	a.m.	
9:00	a.m.	
10:00	a.m.	
11:00	a.m.	
12:00	p.m.	
1:00	p.m.	
2:00	p.m.	
3:00	p.m.	
4:00	p.m.	
5:00	p.m.	
6:00	p.m.	
7:00	p.m.	
8:00	p.m.	
9:00	p.m.	
10:00	p.m.	
11:00	p.m.	
12:00	a.m.	

Daily Plan for Thursday, October 22, 2015

12:00	a.m.	
1:00	a.m.	
2:00	a.m.	
3:00	a.m.	
4:00	a.m.	
5:00	a.m.	
6:00	a.m.	
7:00	a.m.	
8:00	a.m.	
9:00	a.m.	
10:00	a.m.	
11:00	a.m.	
12:00	p.m.	
1:00	p.m.	
2:00	p.m.	
3:00	p.m.	
4:00	p.m.	
5:00	p.m.	
6:00	p.m.	
7:00	p.m.	
8:00	p.m.	
9:00	p.m.	
10:00	p.m.	
11:00	p.m.	
12:00	a.m.	

Daily Plan for Friday, October 23, 2015

12:00	a.m.	
1:00	a.m.	
2:00	a.m.	
3:00	a.m.	
4:00	a.m.	
5:00	a.m.	
6:00	a.m.	
7:00	a.m.	
8:00	a.m.	
9:00	a.m.	
10:00	a.m.	
11:00	a.m.	
12:00	p.m.	
1:00	p.m.	
2:00	p.m.	
3:00	p.m.	
4:00	p.m.	
5:00	p.m.	
6:00	p.m.	
7:00	p.m.	
8:00	p.m.	
9:00	p.m.	
10:00	p.m.	
11:00	p.m.	
12:00	a.m.	

Daily Plan for Saturday, October 24, 2015

Time		
12:00	a.m.	
1:00	a.m.	
2:00	a.m.	
3:00	a.m.	
4:00	a.m.	
5:00	a.m.	
6:00	a.m.	
7:00	a.m.	
8:00	a.m.	
9:00	a.m.	
10:00	a.m.	
11:00	a.m.	
12:00	p.m.	
1:00	p.m.	
2:00	p.m.	
3:00	p.m.	
4:00	p.m.	
5:00	p.m.	
6:00	p.m.	
7:00	p.m.	
8:00	p.m.	
9:00	p.m.	
10:00	p.m.	
11:00	p.m.	
12:00	a.m.	

Daily Plan for Sunday, October 25, 2015

Time		
12:00	a.m.	
1:00	a.m.	
2:00	a.m.	
3:00	a.m.	
4:00	a.m.	
5:00	a.m.	
6:00	a.m.	
7:00	a.m.	
8:00	a.m.	
9:00	a.m.	
10:00	a.m.	
11:00	a.m.	
12:00	p.m.	
1:00	p.m.	
2:00	p.m.	
3:00	p.m.	
4:00	p.m.	
5:00	p.m.	
6:00	p.m.	
7:00	p.m.	
8:00	p.m.	
9:00	p.m.	
10:00	p.m.	
11:00	p.m.	
12:00	a.m.	

Daily Plan for Monday, October 26, 2015

12:00	a.m.	
1:00	a.m.	
2:00	a.m.	
3:00	a.m.	
4:00	a.m.	
5:00	a.m.	
6:00	a.m.	
7:00	a.m.	
8:00	a.m.	
9:00	a.m.	
10:00	a.m.	
11:00	a.m.	
12:00	p.m.	
1:00	p.m.	
2:00	p.m.	
3:00	p.m.	
4:00	p.m.	
5:00	p.m.	
6:00	p.m.	
7:00	p.m.	
8:00	p.m.	
9:00	p.m.	
10:00	p.m.	
11:00	p.m.	
12:00	a.m.	

Daily Plan for Tuesday, October 27, 2015

12:00	a.m.	
1:00	a.m.	
2:00	a.m.	
3:00	a.m.	
4:00	a.m.	
5:00	a.m.	
6:00	a.m.	
7:00	a.m.	
8:00	a.m.	
9:00	a.m.	
10:00	a.m.	
11:00	a.m.	
12:00	p.m.	
1:00	p.m.	
2:00	p.m.	
3:00	p.m.	
4:00	p.m.	
5:00	p.m.	
6:00	p.m.	
7:00	p.m.	
8:00	p.m.	
9:00	p.m.	
10:00	p.m.	
11:00	p.m.	
12:00	a.m.	

Daily Plan for Wednesday, October 28, 2015

12:00	a.m.	
1:00	a.m.	
2:00	a.m.	
3:00	a.m.	
4:00	a.m.	
5:00	a.m.	
6:00	a.m.	
7:00	a.m.	
8:00	a.m.	
9:00	a.m.	
10:00	a.m.	
11:00	a.m.	
12:00	p.m.	
1:00	p.m.	
2:00	p.m.	
3:00	p.m.	
4:00	p.m.	
5:00	p.m.	
6:00	p.m.	
7:00	p.m.	
8:00	p.m.	
9:00	p.m.	
10:00	p.m.	
11:00	p.m.	
12:00	a.m.	

Daily Plan for Thursday, October 29, 2015

12:00	a.m.	
1:00	a.m.	
2:00	a.m.	
3:00	a.m.	
4:00	a.m.	
5:00	a.m.	
6:00	a.m.	
7:00	a.m.	
8:00	a.m.	
9:00	a.m.	
10:00	a.m.	
11:00	a.m.	
12:00	p.m.	
1:00	p.m.	
2:00	p.m.	
3:00	p.m.	
4:00	p.m.	
5:00	p.m.	
6:00	p.m.	
7:00	p.m.	
8:00	p.m.	
9:00	p.m.	
10:00	p.m.	
11:00	p.m.	
12:00	a.m.	

Daily Plan for Friday, October 30, 2015

12:00	a.m.	
1:00	a.m.	
2:00	a.m.	
3:00	a.m.	
4:00	a.m.	
5:00	a.m.	
6:00	a.m.	
7:00	a.m.	
8:00	a.m.	
9:00	a.m.	
10:00	a.m.	
11:00	a.m.	
12:00	p.m.	
1:00	p.m.	
2:00	p.m.	
3:00	p.m.	
4:00	p.m.	
5:00	p.m.	
6:00	p.m.	
7:00	p.m.	
8:00	p.m.	
9:00	p.m.	
10:00	p.m.	
11:00	p.m.	
12:00	a.m.	

Daily Plan for Saturday, October 31, 2015

12:00	a.m.	
1:00	a.m.	
2:00	a.m.	
3:00	a.m.	
4:00	a.m.	
5:00	a.m.	
6:00	a.m.	
7:00	a.m.	
8:00	a.m.	
9:00	a.m.	
10:00	a.m.	
11:00	a.m.	
12:00	p.m.	
1:00	p.m.	
2:00	p.m.	
3:00	p.m.	
4:00	p.m.	
5:00	p.m.	
6:00	p.m.	
7:00	p.m.	
8:00	p.m.	
9:00	p.m.	
10:00	p.m.	
11:00	p.m.	
12:00	a.m.	

Daily Plan for Sunday, November 1, 2015

12:00	a.m.	
1:00	a.m.	
2:00	a.m.	
3:00	a.m.	
4:00	a.m.	
5:00	a.m.	
6:00	a.m.	
7:00	a.m.	
8:00	a.m.	
9:00	a.m.	
10:00	a.m.	
11:00	a.m.	
12:00	p.m.	
1:00	p.m.	
2:00	p.m.	
3:00	p.m.	
4:00	p.m.	
5:00	p.m.	
6:00	p.m.	
7:00	p.m.	
8:00	p.m.	
9:00	p.m.	
10:00	p.m.	
11:00	p.m.	
12:00	a.m.	

Daily Plan for Monday, November 2, 2015

12:00	a.m.	
1:00	a.m.	
2:00	a.m.	
3:00	a.m.	
4:00	a.m.	
5:00	a.m.	
6:00	a.m.	
7:00	a.m.	
8:00	a.m.	
9:00	a.m.	
10:00	a.m.	
11:00	a.m.	
12:00	p.m.	
1:00	p.m.	
2:00	p.m.	
3:00	p.m.	
4:00	p.m.	
5:00	p.m.	
6:00	p.m.	
7:00	p.m.	
8:00	p.m.	
9:00	p.m.	
10:00	p.m.	
11:00	p.m.	
12:00	a.m.	

Daily Plan for Tuesday, November 3, 2015

Time	
12:00 a.m.	
1:00 a.m.	
2:00 a.m.	
3:00 a.m.	
4:00 a.m.	
5:00 a.m.	
6:00 a.m.	
7:00 a.m.	
8:00 a.m.	
9:00 a.m.	
10:00 a.m.	
11:00 a.m.	
12:00 p.m.	
1:00 p.m.	
2:00 p.m.	
3:00 p.m.	
4:00 p.m.	
5:00 p.m.	
6:00 p.m.	
7:00 p.m.	
8:00 p.m.	
9:00 p.m.	
10:00 p.m.	
11:00 p.m.	
12:00 a.m.	

Daily Plan for Wednesday, November 4, 2015

12:00	a.m.	
1:00	a.m.	
2:00	a.m.	
3:00	a.m.	
4:00	a.m.	
5:00	a.m.	
6:00	a.m.	
7:00	a.m.	
8:00	a.m.	
9:00	a.m.	
10:00	a.m.	
11:00	a.m.	
12:00	p.m.	
1:00	p.m.	
2:00	p.m.	
3:00	p.m.	
4:00	p.m.	
5:00	p.m.	
6:00	p.m.	
7:00	p.m.	
8:00	p.m.	
9:00	p.m.	
10:00	p.m.	
11:00	p.m.	
12:00	a.m.	

Daily Plan for Thursday, November 5, 2015

Time	
12:00 a.m.	
1:00 a.m.	
2:00 a.m.	
3:00 a.m.	
4:00 a.m.	
5:00 a.m.	
6:00 a.m.	
7:00 a.m.	
8:00 a.m.	
9:00 a.m.	
10:00 a.m.	
11:00 a.m.	
12:00 p.m.	
1:00 p.m.	
2:00 p.m.	
3:00 p.m.	
4:00 p.m.	
5:00 p.m.	
6:00 p.m.	
7:00 p.m.	
8:00 p.m.	
9:00 p.m.	
10:00 p.m.	
11:00 p.m.	
12:00 a.m.	

Daily Plan for Friday, November 6, 2015

12:00	a.m.	
1:00	a.m.	
2:00	a.m.	
3:00	a.m.	
4:00	a.m.	
5:00	a.m.	
6:00	a.m.	
7:00	a.m.	
8:00	a.m.	
9:00	a.m.	
10:00	a.m.	
11:00	a.m.	
12:00	p.m.	
1:00	p.m.	
2:00	p.m.	
3:00	p.m.	
4:00	p.m.	
5:00	p.m.	
6:00	p.m.	
7:00	p.m.	
8:00	p.m.	
9:00	p.m.	
10:00	p.m.	
11:00	p.m.	
12:00	a.m.	

Daily Plan for Saturday, November 7, 2015

12:00	a.m.	
1:00	a.m.	
2:00	a.m.	
3:00	a.m.	
4:00	a.m.	
5:00	a.m.	
6:00	a.m.	
7:00	a.m.	
8:00	a.m.	
9:00	a.m.	
10:00	a.m.	
11:00	a.m.	
12:00	p.m.	
1:00	p.m.	
2:00	p.m.	
3:00	p.m.	
4:00	p.m.	
5:00	p.m.	
6:00	p.m.	
7:00	p.m.	
8:00	p.m.	
9:00	p.m.	
10:00	p.m.	
11:00	p.m.	
12:00	a.m.	

Daily Plan for Sunday, November 8, 2015

Time		
12:00	a.m.	
1:00	a.m.	
2:00	a.m.	
3:00	a.m.	
4:00	a.m.	
5:00	a.m.	
6:00	a.m.	
7:00	a.m.	
8:00	a.m.	
9:00	a.m.	
10:00	a.m.	
11:00	a.m.	
12:00	p.m.	
1:00	p.m.	
2:00	p.m.	
3:00	p.m.	
4:00	p.m.	
5:00	p.m.	
6:00	p.m.	
7:00	p.m.	
8:00	p.m.	
9:00	p.m.	
10:00	p.m.	
11:00	p.m.	
12:00	a.m.	

Daily Plan for Monday, November 9, 2015

12:00	a.m.	
1:00	a.m.	
2:00	a.m.	
3:00	a.m.	
4:00	a.m.	
5:00	a.m.	
6:00	a.m.	
7:00	a.m.	
8:00	a.m.	
9:00	a.m.	
10:00	a.m.	
11:00	a.m.	
12:00	p.m.	
1:00	p.m.	
2:00	p.m.	
3:00	p.m.	
4:00	p.m.	
5:00	p.m.	
6:00	p.m.	
7:00	p.m.	
8:00	p.m.	
9:00	p.m.	
10:00	p.m.	
11:00	p.m.	
12:00	a.m.	

Daily Plan for Tuesday, November 10, 2015

12:00	a.m.	
1:00	a.m.	
2:00	a.m.	
3:00	a.m.	
4:00	a.m.	
5:00	a.m.	
6:00	a.m.	
7:00	a.m.	
8:00	a.m.	
9:00	a.m.	
10:00	a.m.	
11:00	a.m.	
12:00	p.m.	
1:00	p.m.	
2:00	p.m.	
3:00	p.m.	
4:00	p.m.	
5:00	p.m.	
6:00	p.m.	
7:00	p.m.	
8:00	p.m.	
9:00	p.m.	
10:00	p.m.	
11:00	p.m.	
12:00	a.m.	

Daily Plan for Wednesday, November 11, 2015

12:00 a.m.	
1:00 a.m.	
2:00 a.m.	
3:00 a.m.	
4:00 a.m.	
5:00 a.m.	
6:00 a.m.	
7:00 a.m.	
8:00 a.m.	
9:00 a.m.	
10:00 a.m.	
11:00 a.m.	
12:00 p.m.	
1:00 p.m.	
2:00 p.m.	
3:00 p.m.	
4:00 p.m.	
5:00 p.m.	
6:00 p.m.	
7:00 p.m.	
8:00 p.m.	
9:00 p.m.	
10:00 p.m.	
11:00 p.m.	
12:00 a.m.	

Daily Plan for Thursday, November 12, 2015

Time		
12:00	a.m.	
1:00	a.m.	
2:00	a.m.	
3:00	a.m.	
4:00	a.m.	
5:00	a.m.	
6:00	a.m.	
7:00	a.m.	
8:00	a.m.	
9:00	a.m.	
10:00	a.m.	
11:00	a.m.	
12:00	p.m.	
1:00	p.m.	
2:00	p.m.	
3:00	p.m.	
4:00	p.m.	
5:00	p.m.	
6:00	p.m.	
7:00	p.m.	
8:00	p.m.	
9:00	p.m.	
10:00	p.m.	
11:00	p.m.	
12:00	a.m.	

Daily Plan for Friday, November 13, 2015

12:00	a.m.	
1:00	a.m.	
2:00	a.m.	
3:00	a.m.	
4:00	a.m.	
5:00	a.m.	
6:00	a.m.	
7:00	a.m.	
8:00	a.m.	
9:00	a.m.	
10:00	a.m.	
11:00	a.m.	
12:00	p.m.	
1:00	p.m.	
2:00	p.m.	
3:00	p.m.	
4:00	p.m.	
5:00	p.m.	
6:00	p.m.	
7:00	p.m.	
8:00	p.m.	
9:00	p.m.	
10:00	p.m.	
11:00	p.m.	
12:00	a.m.	

Daily Plan for Saturday, November 14, 2015

12:00	a.m.	
1:00	a.m.	
2:00	a.m.	
3:00	a.m.	
4:00	a.m.	
5:00	a.m.	
6:00	a.m.	
7:00	a.m.	
8:00	a.m.	
9:00	a.m.	
10:00	a.m.	
11:00	a.m.	
12:00	p.m.	
1:00	p.m.	
2:00	p.m.	
3:00	p.m.	
4:00	p.m.	
5:00	p.m.	
6:00	p.m.	
7:00	p.m.	
8:00	p.m.	
9:00	p.m.	
10:00	p.m.	
11:00	p.m.	
12:00	a.m.	

Daily Plan for Sunday, November 15, 2015

Time	
12:00 a.m.	
1:00 a.m.	
2:00 a.m.	
3:00 a.m.	
4:00 a.m.	
5:00 a.m.	
6:00 a.m.	
7:00 a.m.	
8:00 a.m.	
9:00 a.m.	
10:00 a.m.	
11:00 a.m.	
12:00 p.m.	
1:00 p.m.	
2:00 p.m.	
3:00 p.m.	
4:00 p.m.	
5:00 p.m.	
6:00 p.m.	
7:00 p.m.	
8:00 p.m.	
9:00 p.m.	
10:00 p.m.	
11:00 p.m.	
12:00 a.m.	

Daily Plan for Monday, November 16, 2015

12:00	a.m.	
1:00	a.m.	
2:00	a.m.	
3:00	a.m.	
4:00	a.m.	
5:00	a.m.	
6:00	a.m.	
7:00	a.m.	
8:00	a.m.	
9:00	a.m.	
10:00	a.m.	
11:00	a.m.	
12:00	p.m.	
1:00	p.m.	
2:00	p.m.	
3:00	p.m.	
4:00	p.m.	
5:00	p.m.	
6:00	p.m.	
7:00	p.m.	
8:00	p.m.	
9:00	p.m.	
10:00	p.m.	
11:00	p.m.	
12:00	a.m.	

Daily Plan for Tuesday, November 17, 2015

Time		
12:00	a.m.	
1:00	a.m.	
2:00	a.m.	
3:00	a.m.	
4:00	a.m.	
5:00	a.m.	
6:00	a.m.	
7:00	a.m.	
8:00	a.m.	
9:00	a.m.	
10:00	a.m.	
11:00	a.m.	
12:00	p.m.	
1:00	p.m.	
2:00	p.m.	
3:00	p.m.	
4:00	p.m.	
5:00	p.m.	
6:00	p.m.	
7:00	p.m.	
8:00	p.m.	
9:00	p.m.	
10:00	p.m.	
11:00	p.m.	
12:00	a.m.	

Daily Plan for Wednesday, November 18, 2015

12:00	a.m.	
1:00	a.m.	
2:00	a.m.	
3:00	a.m.	
4:00	a.m.	
5:00	a.m.	
6:00	a.m.	
7:00	a.m.	
8:00	a.m.	
9:00	a.m.	
10:00	a.m.	
11:00	a.m.	
12:00	p.m.	
1:00	p.m.	
2:00	p.m.	
3:00	p.m.	
4:00	p.m.	
5:00	p.m.	
6:00	p.m.	
7:00	p.m.	
8:00	p.m.	
9:00	p.m.	
10:00	p.m.	
11:00	p.m.	
12:00	a.m.	

Daily Plan for Thursday, November 19, 2015

12:00	a.m.	
1:00	a.m.	
2:00	a.m.	
3:00	a.m.	
4:00	a.m.	
5:00	a.m.	
6:00	a.m.	
7:00	a.m.	
8:00	a.m.	
9:00	a.m.	
10:00	a.m.	
11:00	a.m.	
12:00	p.m.	
1:00	p.m.	
2:00	p.m.	
3:00	p.m.	
4:00	p.m.	
5:00	p.m.	
6:00	p.m.	
7:00	p.m.	
8:00	p.m.	
9:00	p.m.	
10:00	p.m.	
11:00	p.m.	
12:00	a.m.	

Daily Plan for Friday, November 20, 2015

12:00	a.m.	
1:00	a.m.	
2:00	a.m.	
3:00	a.m.	
4:00	a.m.	
5:00	a.m.	
6:00	a.m.	
7:00	a.m.	
8:00	a.m.	
9:00	a.m.	
10:00	a.m.	
11:00	a.m.	
12:00	p.m.	
1:00	p.m.	
2:00	p.m.	
3:00	p.m.	
4:00	p.m.	
5:00	p.m.	
6:00	p.m.	
7:00	p.m.	
8:00	p.m.	
9:00	p.m.	
10:00	p.m.	
11:00	p.m.	
12:00	a.m.	

Daily Plan for Saturday, November 21, 2015

Time	
12:00 a.m.	
1:00 a.m.	
2:00 a.m.	
3:00 a.m.	
4:00 a.m.	
5:00 a.m.	
6:00 a.m.	
7:00 a.m.	
8:00 a.m.	
9:00 a.m.	
10:00 a.m.	
11:00 a.m.	
12:00 p.m.	
1:00 p.m.	
2:00 p.m.	
3:00 p.m.	
4:00 p.m.	
5:00 p.m.	
6:00 p.m.	
7:00 p.m.	
8:00 p.m.	
9:00 p.m.	
10:00 p.m.	
11:00 p.m.	
12:00 a.m.	

Daily Plan for Sunday, November 22, 2015

12:00	a.m.	
1:00	a.m.	
2:00	a.m.	
3:00	a.m.	
4:00	a.m.	
5:00	a.m.	
6:00	a.m.	
7:00	a.m.	
8:00	a.m.	
9:00	a.m.	
10:00	a.m.	
11:00	a.m.	
12:00	p.m.	
1:00	p.m.	
2:00	p.m.	
3:00	p.m.	
4:00	p.m.	
5:00	p.m.	
6:00	p.m.	
7:00	p.m.	
8:00	p.m.	
9:00	p.m.	
10:00	p.m.	
11:00	p.m.	
12:00	a.m.	

Daily Plan for Monday, November 23, 2015

Time	
12:00	a.m.
1:00	a.m.
2:00	a.m.
3:00	a.m.
4:00	a.m.
5:00	a.m.
6:00	a.m.
7:00	a.m.
8:00	a.m.
9:00	a.m.
10:00	a.m.
11:00	a.m.
12:00	p.m.
1:00	p.m.
2:00	p.m.
3:00	p.m.
4:00	p.m.
5:00	p.m.
6:00	p.m.
7:00	p.m.
8:00	p.m.
9:00	p.m.
10:00	p.m.
11:00	p.m.
12:00	a.m.

Daily Plan for Tuesday, November 24, 2015

Time	
12:00 a.m.	
1:00 a.m.	
2:00 a.m.	
3:00 a.m.	
4:00 a.m.	
5:00 a.m.	
6:00 a.m.	
7:00 a.m.	
8:00 a.m.	
9:00 a.m.	
10:00 a.m.	
11:00 a.m.	
12:00 p.m.	
1:00 p.m.	
2:00 p.m.	
3:00 p.m.	
4:00 p.m.	
5:00 p.m.	
6:00 p.m.	
7:00 p.m.	
8:00 p.m.	
9:00 p.m.	
10:00 p.m.	
11:00 p.m.	
12:00 a.m.	

Daily Plan for Wednesday, November 25, 2015

12:00	a.m.	
1:00	a.m.	
2:00	a.m.	
3:00	a.m.	
4:00	a.m.	
5:00	a.m.	
6:00	a.m.	
7:00	a.m.	
8:00	a.m.	
9:00	a.m.	
10:00	a.m.	
11:00	a.m.	
12:00	p.m.	
1:00	p.m.	
2:00	p.m.	
3:00	p.m.	
4:00	p.m.	
5:00	p.m.	
6:00	p.m.	
7:00	p.m.	
8:00	p.m.	
9:00	p.m.	
10:00	p.m.	
11:00	p.m.	
12:00	a.m.	

Daily Plan for Thursday, November 26, 2015

12:00	a.m.	
1:00	a.m.	
2:00	a.m.	
3:00	a.m.	
4:00	a.m.	
5:00	a.m.	
6:00	a.m.	
7:00	a.m.	
8:00	a.m.	
9:00	a.m.	
10:00	a.m.	
11:00	a.m.	
12:00	p.m.	
1:00	p.m.	
2:00	p.m.	
3:00	p.m.	
4:00	p.m.	
5:00	p.m.	
6:00	p.m.	
7:00	p.m.	
8:00	p.m.	
9:00	p.m.	
10:00	p.m.	
11:00	p.m.	
12:00	a.m.	

Daily Plan for Friday, November 27, 2015

12:00	a.m.	
1:00	a.m.	
2:00	a.m.	
3:00	a.m.	
4:00	a.m.	
5:00	a.m.	
6:00	a.m.	
7:00	a.m.	
8:00	a.m.	
9:00	a.m.	
10:00	a.m.	
11:00	a.m.	
12:00	p.m.	
1:00	p.m.	
2:00	p.m.	
3:00	p.m.	
4:00	p.m.	
5:00	p.m.	
6:00	p.m.	
7:00	p.m.	
8:00	p.m.	
9:00	p.m.	
10:00	p.m.	
11:00	p.m.	
12:00	a.m.	

Daily Plan for Saturday, November 28, 2015

12:00	a.m.	
1:00	a.m.	
2:00	a.m.	
3:00	a.m.	
4:00	a.m.	
5:00	a.m.	
6:00	a.m.	
7:00	a.m.	
8:00	a.m.	
9:00	a.m.	
10:00	a.m.	
11:00	a.m.	
12:00	p.m.	
1:00	p.m.	
2:00	p.m.	
3:00	p.m.	
4:00	p.m.	
5:00	p.m.	
6:00	p.m.	
7:00	p.m.	
8:00	p.m.	
9:00	p.m.	
10:00	p.m.	
11:00	p.m.	
12:00	a.m.	

Daily Plan for Sunday, November 29, 2015

Time		
12:00	a.m.	
1:00	a.m.	
2:00	a.m.	
3:00	a.m.	
4:00	a.m.	
5:00	a.m.	
6:00	a.m.	
7:00	a.m.	
8:00	a.m.	
9:00	a.m.	
10:00	a.m.	
11:00	a.m.	
12:00	p.m.	
1:00	p.m.	
2:00	p.m.	
3:00	p.m.	
4:00	p.m.	
5:00	p.m.	
6:00	p.m.	
7:00	p.m.	
8:00	p.m.	
9:00	p.m.	
10:00	p.m.	
11:00	p.m.	
12:00	a.m.	

Daily Plan for Monday, November 30, 2015

12:00	a.m.	
1:00	a.m.	
2:00	a.m.	
3:00	a.m.	
4:00	a.m.	
5:00	a.m.	
6:00	a.m.	
7:00	a.m.	
8:00	a.m.	
9:00	a.m.	
10:00	a.m.	
11:00	a.m.	
12:00	p.m.	
1:00	p.m.	
2:00	p.m.	
3:00	p.m.	
4:00	p.m.	
5:00	p.m.	
6:00	p.m.	
7:00	p.m.	
8:00	p.m.	
9:00	p.m.	
10:00	p.m.	
11:00	p.m.	
12:00	a.m.	

Daily Plan for Tuesday, December 1, 2015

12:00	a.m.	
1:00	a.m.	
2:00	a.m.	
3:00	a.m.	
4:00	a.m.	
5:00	a.m.	
6:00	a.m.	
7:00	a.m.	
8:00	a.m.	
9:00	a.m.	
10:00	a.m.	
11:00	a.m.	
12:00	p.m.	
1:00	p.m.	
2:00	p.m.	
3:00	p.m.	
4:00	p.m.	
5:00	p.m.	
6:00	p.m.	
7:00	p.m.	
8:00	p.m.	
9:00	p.m.	
10:00	p.m.	
11:00	p.m.	
12:00	a.m.	

Daily Plan for Wednesday, December 2, 2015

12:00	a.m.	
1:00	a.m.	
2:00	a.m.	
3:00	a.m.	
4:00	a.m.	
5:00	a.m.	
6:00	a.m.	
7:00	a.m.	
8:00	a.m.	
9:00	a.m.	
10:00	a.m.	
11:00	a.m.	
12:00	p.m.	
1:00	p.m.	
2:00	p.m.	
3:00	p.m.	
4:00	p.m.	
5:00	p.m.	
6:00	p.m.	
7:00	p.m.	
8:00	p.m.	
9:00	p.m.	
10:00	p.m.	
11:00	p.m.	
12:00	a.m.	

Daily Plan for Thursday, December 3, 2015

12:00	a.m.	
1:00	a.m.	
2:00	a.m.	
3:00	a.m.	
4:00	a.m.	
5:00	a.m.	
6:00	a.m.	
7:00	a.m.	
8:00	a.m.	
9:00	a.m.	
10:00	a.m.	
11:00	a.m.	
12:00	p.m.	
1:00	p.m.	
2:00	p.m.	
3:00	p.m.	
4:00	p.m.	
5:00	p.m.	
6:00	p.m.	
7:00	p.m.	
8:00	p.m.	
9:00	p.m.	
10:00	p.m.	
11:00	p.m.	
12:00	a.m.	

Daily Plan for Friday, December 4, 2015

12:00	a.m.	
1:00	a.m.	
2:00	a.m.	
3:00	a.m.	
4:00	a.m.	
5:00	a.m.	
6:00	a.m.	
7:00	a.m.	
8:00	a.m.	
9:00	a.m.	
10:00	a.m.	
11:00	a.m.	
12:00	p.m.	
1:00	p.m.	
2:00	p.m.	
3:00	p.m.	
4:00	p.m.	
5:00	p.m.	
6:00	p.m.	
7:00	p.m.	
8:00	p.m.	
9:00	p.m.	
10:00	p.m.	
11:00	p.m.	
12:00	a.m.	

Daily Plan for Saturday, December 5, 2015

12:00	a.m.	
1:00	a.m.	
2:00	a.m.	
3:00	a.m.	
4:00	a.m.	
5:00	a.m.	
6:00	a.m.	
7:00	a.m.	
8:00	a.m.	
9:00	a.m.	
10:00	a.m.	
11:00	a.m.	
12:00	p.m.	
1:00	p.m.	
2:00	p.m.	
3:00	p.m.	
4:00	p.m.	
5:00	p.m.	
6:00	p.m.	
7:00	p.m.	
8:00	p.m.	
9:00	p.m.	
10:00	p.m.	
11:00	p.m.	
12:00	a.m.	

Daily Plan for Sunday, December 6, 2015

12:00	a.m.	
1:00	a.m.	
2:00	a.m.	
3:00	a.m.	
4:00	a.m.	
5:00	a.m.	
6:00	a.m.	
7:00	a.m.	
8:00	a.m.	
9:00	a.m.	
10:00	a.m.	
11:00	a.m.	
12:00	p.m.	
1:00	p.m.	
2:00	p.m.	
3:00	p.m.	
4:00	p.m.	
5:00	p.m.	
6:00	p.m.	
7:00	p.m.	
8:00	p.m.	
9:00	p.m.	
10:00	p.m.	
11:00	p.m.	
12:00	a.m.	

Daily Plan for Monday, December 7, 2015

Time		
12:00	a.m.	
1:00	a.m.	
2:00	a.m.	
3:00	a.m.	
4:00	a.m.	
5:00	a.m.	
6:00	a.m.	
7:00	a.m.	
8:00	a.m.	
9:00	a.m.	
10:00	a.m.	
11:00	a.m.	
12:00	p.m.	
1:00	p.m.	
2:00	p.m.	
3:00	p.m.	
4:00	p.m.	
5:00	p.m.	
6:00	p.m.	
7:00	p.m.	
8:00	p.m.	
9:00	p.m.	
10:00	p.m.	
11:00	p.m.	
12:00	a.m.	

Daily Plan for Tuesday, December 8, 2015

12:00	a.m.	
1:00	a.m.	
2:00	a.m.	
3:00	a.m.	
4:00	a.m.	
5:00	a.m.	
6:00	a.m.	
7:00	a.m.	
8:00	a.m.	
9:00	a.m.	
10:00	a.m.	
11:00	a.m.	
12:00	p.m.	
1:00	p.m.	
2:00	p.m.	
3:00	p.m.	
4:00	p.m.	
5:00	p.m.	
6:00	p.m.	
7:00	p.m.	
8:00	p.m.	
9:00	p.m.	
10:00	p.m.	
11:00	p.m.	
12:00	a.m.	

Daily Plan for Wednesday, December 9, 2015

Time		
12:00	a.m.	
1:00	a.m.	
2:00	a.m.	
3:00	a.m.	
4:00	a.m.	
5:00	a.m.	
6:00	a.m.	
7:00	a.m.	
8:00	a.m.	
9:00	a.m.	
10:00	a.m.	
11:00	a.m.	
12:00	p.m.	
1:00	p.m.	
2:00	p.m.	
3:00	p.m.	
4:00	p.m.	
5:00	p.m.	
6:00	p.m.	
7:00	p.m.	
8:00	p.m.	
9:00	p.m.	
10:00	p.m.	
11:00	p.m.	
12:00	a.m.	

Daily Plan for Thursday, December 10, 2015

12:00	a.m.	
1:00	a.m.	
2:00	a.m.	
3:00	a.m.	
4:00	a.m.	
5:00	a.m.	
6:00	a.m.	
7:00	a.m.	
8:00	a.m.	
9:00	a.m.	
10:00	a.m.	
11:00	a.m.	
12:00	p.m.	
1:00	p.m.	
2:00	p.m.	
3:00	p.m.	
4:00	p.m.	
5:00	p.m.	
6:00	p.m.	
7:00	p.m.	
8:00	p.m.	
9:00	p.m.	
10:00	p.m.	
11:00	p.m.	
12:00	a.m.	

Daily Plan for Friday, December 11, 2015

12:00	a.m.	
1:00	a.m.	
2:00	a.m.	
3:00	a.m.	
4:00	a.m.	
5:00	a.m.	
6:00	a.m.	
7:00	a.m.	
8:00	a.m.	
9:00	a.m.	
10:00	a.m.	
11:00	a.m.	
12:00	p.m.	
1:00	p.m.	
2:00	p.m.	
3:00	p.m.	
4:00	p.m.	
5:00	p.m.	
6:00	p.m.	
7:00	p.m.	
8:00	p.m.	
9:00	p.m.	
10:00	p.m.	
11:00	p.m.	
12:00	a.m.	

Daily Plan for Saturday, December 12, 2015

Time	
12:00 a.m.	
1:00 a.m.	
2:00 a.m.	
3:00 a.m.	
4:00 a.m.	
5:00 a.m.	
6:00 a.m.	
7:00 a.m.	
8:00 a.m.	
9:00 a.m.	
10:00 a.m.	
11:00 a.m.	
12:00 p.m.	
1:00 p.m.	
2:00 p.m.	
3:00 p.m.	
4:00 p.m.	
5:00 p.m.	
6:00 p.m.	
7:00 p.m.	
8:00 p.m.	
9:00 p.m.	
10:00 p.m.	
11:00 p.m.	
12:00 a.m.	

Daily Plan for Sunday, December 13, 2015

12:00	a.m.	
1:00	a.m.	
2:00	a.m.	
3:00	a.m.	
4:00	a.m.	
5:00	a.m.	
6:00	a.m.	
7:00	a.m.	
8:00	a.m.	
9:00	a.m.	
10:00	a.m.	
11:00	a.m.	
12:00	p.m.	
1:00	p.m.	
2:00	p.m.	
3:00	p.m.	
4:00	p.m.	
5:00	p.m.	
6:00	p.m.	
7:00	p.m.	
8:00	p.m.	
9:00	p.m.	
10:00	p.m.	
11:00	p.m.	
12:00	a.m.	

Daily Plan for Monday, December 14, 2015

12:00	a.m.	
1:00	a.m.	
2:00	a.m.	
3:00	a.m.	
4:00	a.m.	
5:00	a.m.	
6:00	a.m.	
7:00	a.m.	
8:00	a.m.	
9:00	a.m.	
10:00	a.m.	
11:00	a.m.	
12:00	p.m.	
1:00	p.m.	
2:00	p.m.	
3:00	p.m.	
4:00	p.m.	
5:00	p.m.	
6:00	p.m.	
7:00	p.m.	
8:00	p.m.	
9:00	p.m.	
10:00	p.m.	
11:00	p.m.	
12:00	a.m.	

Daily Plan for Tuesday, December 15, 2015

Time	
12:00 a.m.	
1:00 a.m.	
2:00 a.m.	
3:00 a.m.	
4:00 a.m.	
5:00 a.m.	
6:00 a.m.	
7:00 a.m.	
8:00 a.m.	
9:00 a.m.	
10:00 a.m.	
11:00 a.m.	
12:00 p.m.	
1:00 p.m.	
2:00 p.m.	
3:00 p.m.	
4:00 p.m.	
5:00 p.m.	
6:00 p.m.	
7:00 p.m.	
8:00 p.m.	
9:00 p.m.	
10:00 p.m.	
11:00 p.m.	
12:00 a.m.	

Daily Plan for Wednesday, December 16, 2015

12:00	a.m.	
1:00	a.m.	
2:00	a.m.	
3:00	a.m.	
4:00	a.m.	
5:00	a.m.	
6:00	a.m.	
7:00	a.m.	
8:00	a.m.	
9:00	a.m.	
10:00	a.m.	
11:00	a.m.	
12:00	p.m.	
1:00	p.m.	
2:00	p.m.	
3:00	p.m.	
4:00	p.m.	
5:00	p.m.	
6:00	p.m.	
7:00	p.m.	
8:00	p.m.	
9:00	p.m.	
10:00	p.m.	
11:00	p.m.	
12:00	a.m.	

Daily Plan for Thursday, December 17, 2015

Time	
12:00 a.m.	
1:00 a.m.	
2:00 a.m.	
3:00 a.m.	
4:00 a.m.	
5:00 a.m.	
6:00 a.m.	
7:00 a.m.	
8:00 a.m.	
9:00 a.m.	
10:00 a.m.	
11:00 a.m.	
12:00 p.m.	
1:00 p.m.	
2:00 p.m.	
3:00 p.m.	
4:00 p.m.	
5:00 p.m.	
6:00 p.m.	
7:00 p.m.	
8:00 p.m.	
9:00 p.m.	
10:00 p.m.	
11:00 p.m.	
12:00 a.m.	

Daily Plan for Friday, December 18, 2015

12:00	a.m.	
1:00	a.m.	
2:00	a.m.	
3:00	a.m.	
4:00	a.m.	
5:00	a.m.	
6:00	a.m.	
7:00	a.m.	
8:00	a.m.	
9:00	a.m.	
10:00	a.m.	
11:00	a.m.	
12:00	p.m.	
1:00	p.m.	
2:00	p.m.	
3:00	p.m.	
4:00	p.m.	
5:00	p.m.	
6:00	p.m.	
7:00	p.m.	
8:00	p.m.	
9:00	p.m.	
10:00	p.m.	
11:00	p.m.	
12:00	a.m.	

Daily Plan for Saturday, December 19, 2015

12:00	a.m.	
1:00	a.m.	
2:00	a.m.	
3:00	a.m.	
4:00	a.m.	
5:00	a.m.	
6:00	a.m.	
7:00	a.m.	
8:00	a.m.	
9:00	a.m.	
10:00	a.m.	
11:00	a.m.	
12:00	p.m.	
1:00	p.m.	
2:00	p.m.	
3:00	p.m.	
4:00	p.m.	
5:00	p.m.	
6:00	p.m.	
7:00	p.m.	
8:00	p.m.	
9:00	p.m.	
10:00	p.m.	
11:00	p.m.	
12:00	a.m.	

Daily Plan for Sunday, December 20, 2015

12:00	a.m.	
1:00	a.m.	
2:00	a.m.	
3:00	a.m.	
p4:00	a.m.	
5:00	a.m.	
6:00	a.m.	
7:00	a.m.	
8:00	a.m.	
9:00	a.m.	
10:00	a.m.	
11:00	a.m.	
12:00	p.m.	
1:00	p.m.	
2:00	p.m.	
3:00	p.m.	
4:00	p.m.	
5:00	p.m.	
6:00	p.m.	
7:00	p.m.	
8:00	p.m.	
9:00	p.m.	
10:00	p.m.	
11:00	p.m.	
12:00	a.m.	

Daily Plan for Monday, December 21, 2015

12:00	a.m.	
1:00	a.m.	
2:00	a.m.	
3:00	a.m.	
4:00	a.m.	
5:00	a.m.	
6:00	a.m.	
7:00	a.m.	
8:00	a.m.	
9:00	a.m.	
10:00	a.m.	
11:00	a.m.	
12:00	p.m.	
1:00	p.m.	
2:00	p.m.	
3:00	p.m.	
4:00	p.m.	
5:00	p.m.	
6:00	p.m.	
7:00	p.m.	
8:00	p.m.	
9:00	p.m.	
10:00	p.m.	
11:00	p.m.	
12:00	a.m.	

Daily Plan for Tuesday, December 22, 2015

12:00	a.m.	
1:00	a.m.	
2:00	a.m.	
3:00	a.m.	
4:00	a.m.	
5:00	a.m.	
6:00	a.m.	
7:00	a.m.	
8:00	a.m.	
9:00	a.m.	
10:00	a.m.	
11:00	a.m.	
12:00	p.m.	
1:00	p.m.	
2:00	p.m.	
3:00	p.m.	
4:00	p.m.	
5:00	p.m.	
6:00	p.m.	
7:00	p.m.	
8:00	p.m.	
9:00	p.m.	
10:00	p.m.	
11:00	p.m.	
12:00	a.m.	

Daily Plan for Wednesday, December 23, 2015

Time	
12:00 a.m.	
1:00 a.m.	
2:00 a.m.	
3:00 a.m.	
4:00 a.m.	
5:00 a.m.	
6:00 a.m.	
7:00 a.m.	
8:00 a.m.	
9:00 a.m.	
10:00 a.m.	
11:00 a.m.	
12:00 p.m.	
1:00 p.m.	
2:00 p.m.	
3:00 p.m.	
4:00 p.m.	
5:00 p.m.	
6:00 p.m.	
7:00 p.m.	
8:00 p.m.	
9:00 p.m.	
10:00 p.m.	
11:00 p.m.	
12:00 a.m.	

Daily Plan for Thursday, December 24, 2015

Time		
12:00	a.m.	
1:00	a.m.	
2:00	a.m.	
3:00	a.m.	
4:00	a.m.	
5:00	a.m.	
6:00	a.m.	
7:00	a.m.	
8:00	a.m.	
9:00	a.m.	
10:00	a.m.	
11:00	a.m.	
12:00	p.m.	
1:00	p.m.	
2:00	p.m.	
3:00	p.m.	
4:00	p.m.	
5:00	p.m.	
6:00	p.m.	
7:00	p.m.	
8:00	p.m.	
9:00	p.m.	
10:00	p.m.	
11:00	p.m.	
12:00	a.m.	

Daily Plan for Friday, December 25, 2015

12:00	a.m.	
1:00	a.m.	
2:00	a.m.	
3:00	a.m.	
4:00	a.m.	
5:00	a.m.	
6:00	a.m.	
7:00	a.m.	
8:00	a.m.	
9:00	a.m.	
10:00	a.m.	
11:00	a.m.	
12:00	p.m.	
1:00	p.m.	
2:00	p.m.	
3:00	p.m.	
4:00	p.m.	
5:00	p.m.	
6:00	p.m.	
7:00	p.m.	
8:00	p.m.	
9:00	p.m.	
10:00	p.m.	
11:00	p.m.	
12:00	a.m.	

Daily Plan for Saturday, December 26, 2015

Time		
12:00	a.m.	
1:00	a.m.	
2:00	a.m.	
3:00	a.m.	
4:00	a.m.	
5:00	a.m.	
6:00	a.m.	
7:00	a.m.	
8:00	a.m.	
9:00	a.m.	
10:00	a.m.	
11:00	a.m.	
12:00	p.m.	
1:00	p.m.	
2:00	p.m.	
3:00	p.m.	
4:00	p.m.	
5:00	p.m.	
6:00	p.m.	
7:00	p.m.	
8:00	p.m.	
9:00	p.m.	
10:00	p.m.	
11:00	p.m.	
12:00	a.m.	

Daily Plan for Sunday, December 27, 2015

Time		
12:00	a.m.	
1:00	a.m.	
2:00	a.m.	
3:00	a.m.	
4:00	a.m.	
5:00	a.m.	
6:00	a.m.	
7:00	a.m.	
8:00	a.m.	
9:00	a.m.	
10:00	a.m.	
11:00	a.m.	
12:00	p.m.	
1:00	p.m.	
2:00	p.m.	
3:00	p.m.	
4:00	p.m.	
5:00	p.m.	
6:00	p.m.	
7:00	p.m.	
8:00	p.m.	
9:00	p.m.	
10:00	p.m.	
11:00	p.m.	
12:00	a.m.	

Daily Plan for Monday, December 28, 2015

12:00	a.m.	
1:00	a.m.	
2:00	a.m.	
3:00	a.m.	
4:00	a.m.	
5:00	a.m.	
6:00	a.m.	
7:00	a.m.	
8:00	a.m.	
9:00	a.m.	
10:00	a.m.	
11:00	a.m.	
12:00	p.m.	
1:00	p.m.	
2:00	p.m.	
3:00	p.m.	
4:00	p.m.	
5:00	p.m.	
6:00	p.m.	
7:00	p.m.	
8:00	p.m.	
9:00	p.m.	
10:00	p.m.	
11:00	p.m.	
12:00	a.m.	

Daily Plan for Tuesday, December 29, 2015

12:00	a.m.	
1:00	a.m.	
2:00	a.m.	
3:00	a.m.	
4:00	a.m.	
5:00	a.m.	
6:00	a.m.	
7:00	a.m.	
8:00	a.m.	
9:00	a.m.	
10:00	a.m.	
11:00	a.m.	
12:00	p.m.	
1:00	p.m.	
2:00	p.m.	
3:00	p.m.	
4:00	p.m.	
5:00	p.m.	
6:00	p.m.	
7:00	p.m.	
8:00	p.m.	
9:00	p.m.	
10:00	p.m.	
11:00	p.m.	
12:00	a.m.	

Daily Plan for Wednesday, December 30, 2015

Time		
12:00	a.m.	
1:00	a.m.	
2:00	a.m.	
3:00	a.m.	
4:00	a.m.	
5:00	a.m.	
6:00	a.m.	
7:00	a.m.	
8:00	a.m.	
9:00	a.m.	
10:00	a.m.	
11:00	a.m.	
12:00	p.m.	
1:00	p.m.	
2:00	p.m.	
3:00	p.m.	
4:00	p.m.	
5:00	p.m.	
6:00	p.m.	
7:00	p.m.	
8:00	p.m.	
9:00	p.m.	
10:00	p.m.	
11:00	p.m.	
12:00	a.m.	

Daily Plan for Thursday, December 31, 2015

12:00	a.m.	
1:00	a.m.	
2:00	a.m.	
3:00	a.m.	
4:00	a.m.	
5:00	a.m.	
6:00	a.m.	
7:00	a.m.	
8:00	a.m.	
9:00	a.m.	
10:00	a.m.	
11:00	a.m.	
12:00	p.m.	
1:00	p.m.	
2:00	p.m.	
3:00	p.m.	
4:00	p.m.	
5:00	p.m.	
6:00	p.m.	
7:00	p.m.	
8:00	p.m.	
9:00	p.m.	
10:00	p.m.	
11:00	p.m.	
12:00	a.m.	

Daily Plan for Friday, January 1, 2016

12:00	a.m.	
1:00	a.m.	
2:00	a.m.	
3:00	a.m.	
4:00	a.m.	
5:00	a.m.	
6:00	a.m.	
7:00	a.m.	
8:00	a.m.	
9:00	a.m.	
10:00	a.m.	
11:00	a.m.	
12:00	p.m.	
1:00	p.m.	
2:00	p.m.	
3:00	p.m.	
4:00	p.m.	
5:00	p.m.	
6:00	p.m.	
7:00	p.m.	
8:00	p.m.	
9:00	p.m.	
10:00	p.m.	
11:00	p.m.	
12:00	a.m.	

Daily Plan for Saturday, January 2, 2016

12:00	a.m.	
1:00	a.m.	
2:00	a.m.	
3:00	a.m.	
4:00	a.m.	
5:00	a.m.	
6:00	a.m.	
7:00	a.m.	
8:00	a.m.	
9:00	a.m.	
10:00	a.m.	
11:00	a.m.	
12:00	p.m.	
1:00	p.m.	
2:00	p.m.	
3:00	p.m.	
4:00	p.m.	
5:00	p.m.	
6:00	p.m.	
7:00	p.m.	
8:00	p.m.	
9:00	p.m.	
10:00	p.m.	
11:00	p.m.	
12:00	a.m.	

Daily Plan for Sunday, January 3, 2016

Time		
12:00	a.m.	
1:00	a.m.	
2:00	a.m.	
3:00	a.m.	
4:00	a.m.	
5:00	a.m.	
6:00	a.m.	
7:00	a.m.	
8:00	a.m.	
9:00	a.m.	
10:00	a.m.	
11:00	a.m.	
12:00	p.m.	
1:00	p.m.	
2:00	p.m.	
3:00	p.m.	
4:00	p.m.	
5:00	p.m.	
6:00	p.m.	
7:00	p.m.	
8:00	p.m.	
9:00	p.m.	
10:00	p.m.	
11:00	p.m.	
12:00	a.m.	

Part Six
Notes Section

❖ For miscellaneous information
❖ Additional planning space

Notes

Notes

Notes

Notes

Notes

Notes

Notes

Notes

Notes

Notes

www.ingramcontent.com/pod-product-compliance
Lightning Source LLC
Chambersburg PA
CBHW020329270326
41926CB00007B/109